HERO
WORSHIP

HERO WORSHIP

A Twelve Week Journey to *Become More Like Jesus*

BY TROY KENNEDY

Hero Worship:
A Twelve Week Journey to
Become More Like Jesus
Copyright © 2023 by Troy Kennedy

Published by AMG Publishers
6815 Shallowford Road
Chattanooga, Tennessee 37421

ISBN 13: 978-1-61715-586-4
First Printing—March 2023

Cover designed by BookBaby
Editing by Marissa Wold Uhrina, Eden Prairie, MN
Interior design, and typesetting by PerfecType, Nashville, TN

Printed in the United States of America

DEDICATED TO:

For Gwen, my bride, who "enters in" better than anyone I know.
You have Jesus in your eyes.

. . . .

ACKNOWLEDGMENT

A big thanks to Sara Cormany, who gifted her immense talent and insight to the early editing of Hero Worship for Westside Family Church!

Foreword

We have a son named David who was born without a left hand. Everything just below his elbow is missing. When David was around six years old, we were in the back yard playing catch. My goal was to model for him how to catch and throw a ball with only one hand. So, I would take my glove and tuck it under my opposite arm and throw ball to my son. He would catch the ball, tuck his glove under his left arm, pull out the ball and throw it to me.

David's younger brother Stephen had been watching us and decided he wanted to join in. He went to garage to get his glove and came back with a big smile on his face. When I threw the ball to Stephen, a little grounder, he scooped it up in his glove and then did the unexpected. He placed his glove under his opposite arm, pull out the ball and threw it back to me and then placed the glove back on his left hand. Oh, I forgot to tell you, Stephen has two hands.

What was he doing? He was imitating me and his older brother. Why? That's what people do, particularly with individuals we look up to—our heroes. It is how we learn and how we grow.

Ephesians 5:1 gives us this instruction—

Follow God's example, therefore, as dearly loved children and walk in the way of love, just as Christ loved us and gave himself up for us as a fragrant offering and sacrifice to God. (Ephesians 5:1-2)

The Greek word the author used for the word "follow" is "mimatia" where we get our English word "mimic". If we want to live our best lives, we should simply look at how Jesus lived and do that.

That is what Hero Worship is all about. My good friend and colleague, Troy Kennedy has done a masterful job of showing us how Jesus lived his life – how he prayed, how he asked questions, how he rested. . . . But Troy doesn't leave us with just information, he has laid out this book so we can experience it for ourselves; that we might put into practice the pattern of Jesus and so be transformed into his likeness. This, the Bible says, is our pre-destiny—the vision God had for our lives before we were even born. (Romans 8:29)

My admonition to you is to not simply read the words on the page but go all-in. Memorize the scripture, take a shot at the exercises and ideally do it in community. If you do, I promise you will start to look at little more each day like Jesus, our Hero!

Randy Frazee—Pastor and Author of Think, Act, Be Like Jesus

Readers' Comments

Here are what leaders are saying about Hero Worship:

"Everyone's looking for a hero, but earthly heroes always let us down. More than ever, we live in a culture where people are looking for heroes! "Hero Worship" is such an inspiring reminder that there is really only One whose worth emulating in this life and it's the superhero of all super-heroes, Jesus! By looking closely at His life through this book, you will be motivated in a fresh way to be His worshiper and His disciple! Great job, Troy!"

Tommy Walker—International worship leader and recording artist

"I highly recommend this practical devotional as it takes its readers on a 12 week, life changing, study of the the habits and values of Jesus Christ. In these pages Troy Kennedy, my friend and ministry partner, identifies and shows how to apply the disciplines of the greatest of all heroes."

Rick Muchow—Pastor of Worship Arts at Saddleback Church (ret),
Director Of Worship Practicum, California Baptist University

Troy is a worship leader writing about worship, a disciple maker writing about discipleship. Hero Worship will strengthen you for the single greatest goal in our personal growth: becoming more like Jesus. You'll find clear direction for doing what Jesus did in each chapter, and practical help for making it real in the daily exercises.

Tom Holliday—Teaching Pastor, Saddleback Church

"The Hero Worship study for me was a wonderful way to personalize the Word. While I read the Bible, studying it in this way, where it's broken into easy-to-understand messages that allow for reflection and guided study, was so helpful. This made it a very real and personal experience."

Barbara Teicher— CSP Global Leadership Development and Communication Speaker

In "Hero Worship: A 12 Week Journey to Become More Like Jesus" Troy Kennedy offers important insights into the life of Jesus as a way for us to become true worshippers. He gleans lessons that will deepen your understanding of the disciplines surrounding Jesus but powerfully take you into "Worship" and, more importantly, challenge you to rethink the role that your life plays with the people around you. I highly recommend it for you personally or with your small group!

Steve Gladen—Pastor of Small Groups, Saddleback Church, Author of *Leading Small Groups With Purpose*

"I was in the military for over 22 years and have study/read many leadership books and I've tried my best to apply their leadership methods to my life, without any luck. I think this book should be used in many leadership programs throughout corporate America as well as in the military. Jesus' lifestyle is the only lifestyle we should try to copy."

Major Bill Smith—U.S. Army (ret)

"God calls every pastor to a specific vision for ministry. Let Pastor Troy's book take you on a journey and teach you some biblical practices to create space in your life and become more like our Hero Jesus. The pages are full of truth and humor... I couldn't put it down... a fresh way to look at loving Jesus and loving others."

Brad Norman—Next Steps Pastor, Westside Family Church

"Hero Worship for me really came down to the emphasis on the relationship with Jesus. It's not just another Christian "self-help" book that puts the weight of being closer to Jesus on your own ability to execute a set number of tasks or equates ritualistic behaviors with closeness to God. It's much more than that. At the same time, however, it gives you practical examples and outlines of behaviors to incorporate into your daily life that are all designed to draw you closer to Jesus. I truly fell in love with the heart of Hero Worship—that is, that being intentional with giving room to Jesus in your day to day and choosing to engage in some of the outlined practices that Jesus Himself engaged in. It helps bring you to a place of simply beholding Jesus more. It holds practical guidelines and encouraging examples of how to daily practice His presence in your life, which leads you to true closeness with Him."

Dr. Nathaniel Greenwood

"'Hero Worship' has been a wonderful resource that has helped me grow closer to Jesus in practical ways. It's not just theory, but a step-by-step journey in following Jesus!!! Troy is an amazing follower of Christ and this method of daily rhythms of discovering Jesus has been life altering in the best of ways!!!"

Jason Morris—Westside Family Church, Pastor of Global Innovation

Contents

How to Use This Book

This journey is designed to be experienced in weekly increments. You can, of course, use it in whatever rhythm you like. But this is how I suggest you start.

In the first week, you are asked to read the introduction in its entirety. The heart of it will frame your eleven-week journey. In the subsequent weeks, you will find an explanation of each practice as well as how that practice is observed in the life of Jesus and how it can be incorporated into your daily routine. In order to help you with that routine, you will engage in a six-day interactive guide through each discipline.

On each page there is

- a weekly verse to memorize,
- a weekly practice in which to engage,
- a daily verse and questions to help you focus,
- a daily practice suggestion, and
- a daily journal prompt to process the day's experience.

I encourage you to fully engage in each day's practice. Set aside a regular space and time to focus on the practice and journal. This will help you to get all you can out of the experience.

This journey may also be experienced with a group. Each week you can debrief with your group and share how the practice went, as well as review the week's memory verse. Use the focus questions for discussion. What did you learn? Do you have any stories you can share with the others? How did the practice challenge you? What is the upcoming week's practice? How can we be accountable and encouraging to one another to get the most from the following week's practice?

The goal is to get closer to our Hero and become more like Him. If you keep that as your focus, you will find transformation. Remember that each practice is a way to create more space for your relationship with God and with other people. Love, not obligation, is the engine behind the practices. Love should always be the context for us as we follow after Jesus, our Hero.

While this is a starter to the Jesus-like life, remember it is just a beginning. It is in no way meant to be a comprehensive guide to every aspect of Jesus's life and character. We could (and will) spend a lifetime on that journey. For two thousand years, volumes have been written on the life and practices of Jesus, which have evolved in countless ways over church history. But these are the practices that are most directly observable and accessible in the life of Jesus. And out of love and admiration for our Hero, they are where we will start in imitation of Him.

My prayer is that it is a catalyst for you as you grow in intimacy with God and explore the endless depths of beauty, wisdom, and love found in the face of the Savior.

Introduction

Everyone is looking for a hero. Someone to look up to. Someone to imitate. Someone to show us that our lives can matter and that it's all going to be okay. We long to know that someone has faced all life can bring and come out victorious—because heroes give us hope, the hope that somehow we can live the same story.

When we admire someone, we go out of our way to imitate them. Sometimes our imitations are trivial and fun. You got the unfortunate haircut of your favorite musical artist when it was still trendy. You had to wear the jersey number of your basketball hero. You knew you would run faster if Mom and Dad would just buy you that athlete's overpriced, signature shoe. Surely we would attain some degree of greatness and the admiration of our adolescent friends, by our tacet association with these beloved celebrities along with everyone else who did the exact same thing!

Other times, our search to find a hero reeks of desperation. We look to an actor who portrays a character we admire for their courage, humor, and charisma. We hold up a musical artist who has the adoration of our hearts. We look to athletes who perform in competition in ways we can only dream. It may be a wealthy businessperson, a politician, or even a family member who becomes a model for us. The list goes on and on.

Our hearts hunger for someone to show us how we should live our lives. So we intuitively search for someone whose life exemplifies wisdom, joy, courage, honesty, humor, and, most of all, transcendent, selfless love. We long for a hero who shows us that the pain and evil of this world does not have the final say. A hero who brings us hope that tomorrow can be better than today. A hero who lives a life worthy of imitation. And if we can't find someone who fits the bill, we fill it with a lesser substitute. Because let's face it, a counterfeit hero is better than no hero at all.

But the truth is, we don't have to settle. There is someone who has lived the life that shows us that the pain, evil, and suffering of this world do not have the final word. There is someone who is love, purpose, and power. There is someone who is a hero of such humility, character, and sublime wisdom that we stand in awe. Someone who faced accusation, injustice, evil, and buried them all. Someone who is worthy of our adoration and imitation. Someone who gives us hope for tomorrow and strength for today. He is the God-man, Jesus, full of truth and grace.

In Jesus, we have a Hero who asks us to come closer, to walk in His steps, and to breathe the air He breathes. He is the only hero who only grows the closer we get. It is the inverse experience of our human heroes, who often disappoint us when we see the person behind the persona. From a distance, we can see Jesus as a nice guy, a good teacher, a liar, a megalomaniac, or a nut job. But the closer we get, the clearer our vision gets and the more overwhelmed we are with His claims. He is no mortal hero. He is the embodiment of love wrapped in the blood, sweat, and flesh of a man. He is hope where all other hope disappoints—because no hero has ever made the kind of claims Jesus made and remained worthy of our admiration and worship.

Jesus Receives Worship

Jesus is unique in contrast with the leaders of all the major world religions. When people tried to worship Buddha, Krishna, or Mohammad, they were turned away. These leaders would all readily tell their followers that they were just as human as the next person. Perhaps they were more elevated or enlightened humans, but they were self-proclaimed humans, unworthy of worship. In contrast, Jesus readily received worship. He claimed that to know Him, to see Him, and to hear Him was to know, see, and hear God Himself. He forgave sin and claimed He could grant people eternal life. Jesus didn't leave any room for another interpretation. It was either accept Him as God in the flesh or reject Him altogether.

The New Testament authors go out of their way to make this point. As men who knew Jesus firsthand, they also passionately proclaimed His deity:

> The Son is the radiance of God's glory and the exact representation of his being, sustaining all things by his powerful word. (Hebrews 1:3 NIV)

> In the beginning was the Word, and the Word was with God, and the Word was God. He was with God in the beginning. Through him all things were made; without him nothing was made that has been made. . . . The Word became flesh and made his dwelling among us. We have seen his glory, the glory of the one and only Son, who came from the Father, full of grace and truth. (John 1:1–3, 14) NIV

> The Son is the image of the invisible God, the firstborn over all creation. For in him all things were created: things in heaven and on earth, visible and invisible, whether thrones or powers or rulers or authorities; all things have been created through him and for him. He is before all things, and in him all things hold together. . . . For God was pleased to have all his fullness dwell in him." (Colossians 1:15–17, 19 NIV)

It is interesting that at the beginning of each of these books of the Bible the authors go out of their way to establish this truth. There is no gray area. There is no ambiguity or wiggle room. Jesus is God in the flesh, and He is the only being truly worthy of our adoration, submission, and imitation. Everyone else would prove to be a counterfeit or a grave disappointment. Because no one other than Jesus can bear our identities, hopes, and expectations.

All the tiny gods of our world promise much and deliver precious little. We can spin the lazy Susan of tiny gods one after the other in the hope that eventually one will deliver on their promises. But we spin in vain. It is the history of man's desperate experience to worship created things rather than the Creator only to come up empty. When we place our hope in tiny gods, not only are they crushed under the weight of expectation, but we are also crushed in the aftermath. Our hearts will continue to wander until they find their rest in Him, the one true God.

Understanding the Trinity

Only God is worthy of hero worship. And if we want to know what God looks like, all we need to do is look at Jesus because Jesus is the center of all of Scripture and the clearest view we have of God. The better we understand this, the more profound our Hero becomes.

We understand that Jesus has authority because He is God in the flesh and part of what Christians have called the *trinitarian mystery*. God is the great three in one: Father, Son, and Holy Spirit. The Father and the Spirit are fully present in Jesus. Jesus and the Spirit are fully present in the Father. Jesus and the Father are fully present in the Spirit. Think of it like this:

> The fullness of God in Christ,
> The fullness of Christ in the Spirit,
> The fullness of the Spirit alive in us,
> And through His Spirit, we are made fully alive.

If anyone does not have the Spirit of Christ, they do not belong to Christ. But if Christ is in you, then even though your body is subject to death because of sin, the Spirit gives life because of righteousness. (Romans 8:9–10 NIV)

Because you are his sons, God sent the Spirit of his Son into our hearts, the Spirit who calls out, "*Abba*, Father. (Galatians 4:6 NIV)

[Jesus says,] "If you love me, keep my commands. And I will ask the Father, and he will give you another advocate to help you and be with you forever—the Spirit of truth. The world cannot accept him, because it neither sees him nor knows him. But you know him, for he lives with you and will be in you. I will not leave you as orphans; I will come to you." (John 14:15–18 NIV)

Everyone can know Jesus. Everyone can walk in step with His spirit. Everyone can access the Father without some other mediator. He will work in, through, and beyond anyone who seeks Him. That is what "God with us" means for you and me. We are never alone. This Hero is closer than we ever dared dream or imagine.

The Vine and the Branches

Our Hero tells us that it is only by abiding in Him that we can live in the fullness and joy He desires for all of us: "I am the vine; you are the branches. If you remain in me and I in you, you will bear much fruit; apart from me you can do nothing" (John 15:5 NIV). Intimacy with Jesus is the source of nutrition, growth, and fruitfulness. If the branch is separated from the vine, it is fruitless. It withers when it is separated from the source of life and eventually dies. If it remains or abides, it lives fruitfully and abundantly.

Only in cultivating an abiding intimacy with Jesus do we live the transformed Jesus-like life. We must cling to Him, seek Him, desire His presence, and follow hard after Him. In the seeking, He meets us. In the seeking, He sustains us. In the seeking, He lives his life through us and beyond us. That is what "Thy Kingdom come, Thy will be done on earth as it is in heaven" looks like in you and me. It is the Christ-like life lived out and empowered by the Spirit of Jesus, Himself, within us.

He gives us this word picture in the Lord's Prayer from Matthew 6 to help us understand that apart from Him, we can do nothing. We cannot bear the kingdom fruit or live the abundant life of eternal significance our souls so desire without staying close to Him. But in the abiding, the staying, the seeking, and the following we find intimacy with the Savior. Joy is made complete in loving Him and His children.

When we love someone, our lives change. We are willing to compromise on things we would never compromise for acquaintances. We find ourselves going to places we would typically never go, looking at things we would avoid otherwise. Love reshapes the rhythm of our lives in consideration of the one loved. The more we love, the more we are willing to change and progressively become one with each other.

So it is with Jesus. If we want to be more like our Hero, we will get closer to Him. We will not just think loving thoughts. We will express love through action. We will love because He first loved us. And Jesus was clear. The best way we can show our love for Him is to love one another: "This is my command: Love each other" (John 15:17 NIV).

To know Him is to love Him. To love Him is to trust Him. To trust Him is to obey Him joyfully. To obey Him is to love like Him. Over and over Jesus declares, "This is my commandment, that you love one another as I have loved you" (John 15:12 ESV). The fullest way to experience and express the Jesus-like life is to "love one another." And our Hero shows us what that life looks like. He calls us to come close, listen, observe, and imitate Him as any great teacher would. It is not just an education of information but emulation. It is active, kinetic, and tactile. It will get you dirty and uncomfortable. And it will challenge and fulfill you like no other educational endeavor, because it is more than education. It is transformation.

The practices we will engage in throughout this experience are ways of putting action to the impulse. They are more than internal dialogue expressing a fleeting desire for the Jesus-like life. They are concrete practices that intentionally carve out space for a greater love relationship with Him and a greater love relationship with people. As such, it only makes sense that we would look to Jesus as the model of what it looks like to love God and our neighbor.

Practice

Information does not equal transformation. Yes, information is essential. But it is not effective until it is put into practice.

Let's say Michael Phelps is just learning to swim. He is built like a swimmer. He has the innate talent. He has all the gear—goggles, Speedo, and a swim cap. He even has his "win at all costs" attitude. But we find him sitting on the starting platform reading *Swimming for Dummies*. He absorbs the book from front to back, memorizing large portions of it. He even reads it and rereads it for years. But he never jumps in the pool. He never gains speed. He never wins. All that preparation becomes useless because he never gets in the water. How tragic would that be?

In the same way, the point of practicing isn't to get good at practicing. It is to prepare us for something. It puts us in the position to be coached by someone who knows things we don't know. It asks us to exercise a behavior that directly or indirectly changes our automatic responses. And isn't it all about responses?

In the heat of competition, the thousands of hours of practice result in unconscious freedom. The muscles remember the movement as the mind cannot possibly think about every nuance of the shot. It is the freedom of being in the moment without observation or critique. Consider the sinuous beauty of Michael Jordan or LeBron James as they take basketball from sport to more of an art. There is a kinetic, intuitive joy informed by not just talent, but by thousands of shots practiced in driveways, neighborhood courts, and team practices under the watchful eye of a coach.

In the same way, imagine a great jazz musician flowing freely and fluidly from one tonal center to the next as the melodies are created in the moment. All the time locked in his bedroom learning the scales of every key and every mode, all the great influencers like Coltrane and Bird having been absorbed into his musical reservoir and all the tutoring of every music teacher in countless hours of lessons come together in moments of transcendent freedom.

Just as practice creates freedom for the artist, the practice of the Jesus-like life will produce freedom for us. The flow of His Spirit is evidenced in our real-time encounters with life. Intimacy with God always brings transformation from the inside out. It changes us from the kind of person who knows what is good to one who intuitively does what is good.

When we follow after Jesus and practice the things that He practiced, we intentionally put ourselves in a position to meet with Him, be influenced by Him, and ultimately behave more like Him. If Jesus is our hero and our model, we will want to practice what Jesus did in the mundane so that we will respond more like Jesus in the challenge.

These changes don't just occur when we intellectually assent to them. We have to act and meet God in our practice space. When we exercise these practices, we are intentionally saying, "I want to be more like you, and I'm willing to change." As we reach out to God in those moments, He reaches out to us to graciously change us from the inside out while renewing our thoughts, feelings, and character.

At the same time, it behooves us to fix our eyes on Jesus, the author and perfecter of faith. And we must be willing to practice the things that Jesus practiced as His Spirit coaches and shapes us. As He pours out of us more and more, our egos and agendas become less and less. But this doesn't happen without practice. This doesn't happen until we have carved out time to meet with Him and learn His agenda. We have to be willing to change. We have to be willing to be coached. We have to show up to practice.

Practice Space

Practice rooms, weight rooms, basketball courts, libraries, and so on are all spaces designed with intention. They serve a primary purpose. The practice rooms at the music school I attended were noisy places. One could walk down the hall and hear any number of styles of music as busy students practiced their craft. Saxophones peeled off jazz licks. Opera singers struggled with the high notes of a new aria. The piano major tried to master the unbelievably intricate music of Chopin. Even the music education major squeaking through beginning notes on the clarinet was regularly heard as part of the cacophony. People with a wide array of skill levels all sought out that space with the intention of getting just a little bit better in that hour. Add enough of those hours together over time and it would bring freedom in the heat of performance.

Because these rooms were designated for that activity, all that noise was completely appropriate. But take that same beginning clarinetist and place them in the library, which is meant for quiet study, and the previously acceptable activity becomes wildly out of context and disturbing. No one wants to sit next to someone learning the clarinet in the library. Seriously. It simply is not the right place.

Clearly, there is something to be said about finding the appropriate practice space. And as we walk with Jesus, it is helpful not only to carve out space in our schedule, but also to designate a physical space for practice. One that focuses the heart and mind without the distraction and clutter of our lives. It is a place that is primarily intended for that one thing. When we are there, it is practice time. It could be in a car. It could be in a designated room of the house. It could be in a break room at the office. It could even be a prayer closet that has been set aside as practice space. But designating a specific time and place where we will practice the more solitary exercises in this journey will be helpful as we establish these sacred rhythms in our everyday lives.

The goal of this journey is not change. The goal is intimacy with Christ. The goal is to know Jesus better. Because when we seek intimacy over change, we naturally want to be like Him. From that relationship, we gain life from love, abundance from poverty of spirit, and transformation from surrender. It is the well for the thirsty soul. It is the easy yoke He so desires to give us. It is the full gift of grace. Our Hero is the perfect embodiment of who God is and has always been.

Jesus is present and patient, and he is *for* you. He's not looking for you to mess it up. He is eagerly meeting you in that sacred space of life: "He rewards those who earnestly seek him" (Hebrews 11:6 NIV). "Draw near to God, and he will draw near to you" (James 4:8 NIV). As we go to practice and train with Him, there is no condemnation. There is no downside. There is only joy in the ever-growing love relationship we have with our Hero.

Love Is the Context

Love is the context for everything good. When asked what was the most important commandment in Scripture, Jesus replied: "'Love the Lord your God with all your heart and with all your soul and with all your mind.' This is the first and greatest commandment. And the second is like it: 'Love your neighbor as yourself.' All the Law and the Prophets hang on these two commandments" (Matthew 22:37–40 NIV). In other words, love fulfills all the requirements of holiness. Focus on the law, and we get legalism. Focus on love, and we gain God's law as well.

All of the practices we will explore in this journey can be thought of as fulfilling one or both of these overlapping categories. They are ways of cultivating intimacy with God and with people. They are there to create sacred space for love to grow with God and with others. We enter into that area carved out in our lives with purpose and anticipation that the Holy Spirit will meet us and empower us to be the kind of person who does what love requires.

Understand there is grace for the journey. Some of these practices will be intuitive and easy. Some will be quite difficult. But none of them are intended to bring you guilt. We aren't trying to master any particular one. We are intentionally stepping into the grace of becoming more like our Master. Know that every practice need not be exercised all the time and that every practice can be exercised some of the time.

Questions for Reflection

1. Did you have any heroes when you were growing up? What did you do to imitate him or her?

    _____

    _____

    _____

    _____

2. The New Testament authors state clearly that Jesus is the perfect image and embodiment of God. Have you thought of Jesus in that way, or did you see Him in some other way? How does seeing Jesus as equal with God help you in your daily life?

    _____

    _____

    _____

    _____

3. Do you have a hobby or skill that took a great deal of practice to learn? Was there a master of that skill that you saw as an example? Is the imitation of Jesus's practices intimidating for you? Why or why not?

    _____

    _____

    _____

    _____

4. If someone tells you that he or she should be worshipped, what possible conclusions can you draw about him or her?

    _____

    _____

    _____

    _____

5. How are love for and obedience to Jesus related? What is the connection Jesus makes in John 15?

    _____

    _____

    _____

    _____

6. How does love for God and other people summarize and complete the requirements of the Old Testament?

    _____

    _____

    _____

    _____

Jesus Prayed

To be a Christian without prayer is no more possible
than to be alive without breathing.
—Martin Luther

For Jesus, prayer was just as natural and necessary as any other life-giving exercise. At every turn, we encounter Him lifting up His heart to His Father in prayer. This practice was the foundation of His ministry on earth and permeated everything He did. So as we follow in our Hero's footsteps, it only makes sense that prayer will be the first practice we put into place on our journey toward a Jesus-like life.

Prayer in its simplest form is connection with God. It is the intentional cultivation of the relationship with your Creator. It is "spiritual transaction with the Creator of Heaven and Earth," as Charles Spurgeon put it. Prayer encapsulates a hundred different facets of life, and our prayer relationship with God can be complex like any relationship between humans. Throughout the Bible, we see the heroes of Scripture engaging in prayer by crying, laughing, complaining, shouting, whispering, asking, singing, dancing, and at times just listening. Such a wide variety exists because the practice of prayer can run the gambit of human emotion and experience. It happens any time we find God present in our lives and engage Him there.

Jesus often withdrew to lonely places and prayed.

Luke 5:16 NIV

While prayer was practiced by all biblical heroes, it is especially true of our greatest Hero, Jesus. He prayed alone and with others. He prayed over major events and the mundane. He prayed at daybreak, at meals, and, at times, all night long. He prayed in celebration, in temptation, in need, and in gratitude. Prayer was consistently present in every corner of His earthly ministry.

So if we are to start anywhere in following our Hero, we must start with prayer. Just as Jesus found it essential to seek out His heavenly Father in prayer through every circumstance, so must we. It is this transcendent connection with God that will constantly guide and shape us.

One aspect of prayer is unbroken, daily awareness of our relationship with God, what Brother Lawrence, the famous seventeenth-century monk known for his intimacy with God, called "practicing the presence of God." Jesus certainly had this kind of constant conscious connection with the Father. But it is important to note that Jesus set aside time to stop every other activity and focus solely on prayer.

Even the disciples needed His example and instruction: "One day Jesus was praying in a certain place. When he finished, one of his disciples said to him, "Lord, teach us to pray" Luke 11:1 NIV).

Prayer has always been a regular part of Jewish faith and culture. It is modeled throughout the Old Testament, whether in the beauty of Psalms or the pain of Lamentations. But for some reason, when the disciples watched Jesus pray, they knew something was different and it was time to relearn how to pray from Jesus Himself.

He answered their request with the words of Matthew 6:9–13:

"This, then, is how you should pray:
'Our Father in heaven,
hallowed be your name,

your kingdom come,
your will be done,
    on earth as it is in heaven.
Give us today our daily bread.
And forgive us our debts,
    as we also have forgiven our debtors.
And lead us not into temptation,
    but deliver us from the evil one.'"

And later, the early church added, "For your is the kingdom, the power, and the glory forever and ever. Amen."

What a great ending! Even though it isn't precisely what Jesus said, it still honors the heart of Scripture in proclaiming the sovereignty of God. And while we must keep in mind that Jesus didn't intend for it to be said verbatim, it is intended to be a model for us as our prayer lives grow in regular intimacy with Him. As such, we will examine it in its respective parts to shape our budding prayer lives.

Our Father in Heaven

The first thing Jesus tells us is to approach God as a Father—a perfectly good, perfectly loving, heavenly Father. One who knows things we don't know and sees things with an eternal perspective. One who is for us, not against us. One who is a father who looks on us with favor and wants to give us the best life that can be provided by a Dad, who is the Author of life itself.

I once heard a preacher say, "If God had a wallet, your picture would be in it." What a powerful image. God is showing off His picture of you to any angel who stands still long enough to look. And with one zip, the photos come tumbling out with fatherly pride. We are cherished and doted on by a heavenly Daddy who couldn't be more in love with His kids.

So when we pray, let's start there and stay there until it sinks in layer by layer and we know we are extravagantly loved by the Creator of the universe, a proud Daddy who dances over us all in joy.

Hallowed Be Your Name

Names in the ancient world have a much more profound weight than they do for most contemporary cultures. For the ancient Jews, someone's name always had meaning. It contained the essence of their personhood and was nearly synonymous with their identity.

"Hallowed" is an archaic way of saying something is holy, consecrated, or set apart. To say God's name is holy is to say it is like no other name, or rather, it holds a weight that no other name can hold. For the Jew, God's name was so profoundly sacred that it could not be spoken out loud. Prior to transcribing Scripture, scholars would have to bathe in preparation, and when they wrote the name of God, the scribe would clean the pen and wash his entire body in a mikvah, a pool of natural running water.

God's name, YHWH, is translated "Yahweh," "Jehovah," or "Adonai" for different reasons throughout Scripture. When Moses encountered God in the burning bush, His name was translated "I Am that I Am." His name is pure, timeless, and the spiritual essence of being from which all other being is derived. It is also the name Jesus claims for Himself in John 8 when He declares "before Abraham was born, I AM." That Jesus would claim the name of God, the name so sacred that it isn't to be spoken, was hugely offensive to the Jews. In short, Jesus was taking the name that contained all the weight of God's glory for Himself.

When we pray "hallowed be your name," we recognize God's otherness. We are like God in that we are made in His image. But He still precedes and supersedes the natural world in every way. He is the Creator, and we are the created.

Your Kingdom Come, Your Will Be Done

Jesus's primary message in His earthly ministry was that the Kingdom of God was at hand. He likened it to a small seed or to yeast, both things that are small but grow into profound effect. Dallas Willard says one's kingdom is the "range of one's effective will." The Kingdom that Jesus preached is both here and yet to come. It is present all around us and is immediately accessible through Jesus.

When we pray "Your will be done," we are recognizing and submitting to God's authority. It is the surrender of my will to God's will, my kingdom to God's Kingdom. It expresses our heart cry to participate in God's plan for not just our own lives, but for His plan for humanity. It asks, "What is my role? What is my post? What is your Kingdom plan?"

On Earth as It Is in Heaven

The gospel Jesus preached was never about escaping. It was never about leaving this mess behind for the great somewhere up there. The gospel is for all of God's creation and its ultimate redemption. It is "up there" coming "down here." And because we are ambassadors of God's Kingdom, He can bring heaven down here through us and beyond us each and every day.

Give us this Day Our Daily Bread

In this line, we declare our complete dependence on God and trust in Him for everything in our lives. He has given us the capacity to think, create, and engage. He gives us the breath in our lungs and the blood in our veins. Even the opportunities and interactions of life belong to Him. All of life is a grace. And in that, there is contentment for today, just as there will also be contentment for tomorrow.

Forgive Our Debts as We Forgive Our Debtors

Different translations use the words *trespasses* or *sins* in place of *debts*. The heart of it, however, is the same. Jesus tells us that our experience of God's forgiveness is directly related to how we forgive others.

He said to the paralyzed man, "Son, your sins are forgiven." Now some teachers of the law were sitting there, thinking to themselves,

"Why does this fellow talk like that? He's blaspheming! Who can forgive sins but God alone?" (Mark 2:5–7 NIV)

It was considered blasphemy when Jesus forgave the sins of the crippled man because only God can forgive sins. Jesus not only proclaims His deity but He is also telling us that every offense, every injustice, every slander, and every lie aimed at His children is a sin against them and a sin against Himself. He is not a distant bystander. God is a Father who cares intimately and deeply about His children. He takes the offense as well as the debt of forgiveness upon Himself, asking us to do the same.

As we follow after our Hero, Jesus instructs us to forgive as we have been forgiven. And as His forgiveness has been so freely and extravagantly offered to us, so are we to offer our forgiveness freely to those who have hurt us.

And Lead Us Not into Temptation but Deliver Us from the Evil One

Jesus spent forty days being tempted by the evil one in the wilderness. He was offered every category of desire that plagues the human heart, but through fasting, prayer, and Scripture, He overcame the temptations that are common to us all. This was in no way a trivial encounter for Jesus. This was a conflict of cosmic proportion as Jesus stood in the gap for all of humanity. Yes, the enemy was defeated but at great personal cost to our Hero. We may never know the toll it took on Him as He faced down the embodiment of true evil.

Jesus would much rather we never have to experience that kind of costly battle in our own strength. He knows intimately how painful, seductive, and dangerous that encounter can be, so He instructs us to deliberately pray against and actively avoid those temptations that war against our souls. This is a prayer for wisdom and power. Oh God, grant us the resolve and discernment to walk away from darkness and into the light and life you would have for us.

One Last Observation

Notice how Jesus instructs us: "*Our* Father," "Give *us* today," "Forgive *us*," "Lead *us*." Jesus frames this entirely through the lens of collective identity.

Our modern, Western worldview has a difficult time seeing identity as collective. But for the ancient Jew, as well as many contemporary Eastern cultures, this was the primary way people thought of themselves. Identity was always about *us*. In the same way, our family, our tribe, our nation should take precedent in an individual's thinking over just his or her individual identity. Our hearts and minds will experience some much-needed expansion as we begin to see the world through the eyes that see more than our own immediate needs and interests.

For the next week, we will carve out time to pray through the Lord's Prayer. As we follow our Hero, we will not only make prayer a priority, but we will also follow His instruction on how to pray. Then, as the week progresses, we will shift the focus from seeing the prayer through just the lens of our personal lives and refocus it on our relationships with our families, our community, and our country.

Jesus Prayed

MEMORIZE

This, then, is how you should pray:
"Our Father in heaven,
hallowed be your name,
your kingdom come,
your will be done,
on earth as it is in heaven.
Give us today our daily bread.
And forgive us our debts,
as we also have forgiven our debtors.
And lead us not into temptation,
but deliver us from the evil one."
—Matthew 6:9–13 (NIV)

Focus Daily: (Read the above verse.)

Focus Questions: How does seeing God as a Father change the way you pray? Is it more difficult or easier? Why do you think Jesus instructed us to approach God first as a Heavenly Father?

Practice Daily: As we begin, remember your posture in the practice is to create space for intimacy with God. Ask God to help you push aside all the clutter in your mind. Sit and linger with that before you start. Pray through the Lord's Prayer today in regards to your personal relationship with God. Read through each part and ask yourself how it is reflected in your own heart.

JOURNAL DAILY

(Write at least three sentences per day):

_____

_____

_____

_____

_____

_____

_____

_____

_____

_____

_____

_____

_____

_____

_____

Jesus Prayed

MEMORIZE

This, then, is how you should pray:
"Our Father in heaven,
hallowed be your name,
your kingdom come,
your will be done,
on earth as it is in heaven.
Give us today our daily bread.
And forgive us our debts,
as we also have forgiven our debtors.
And lead us not into temptation,
but deliver us from the evil one."
—Matthew 6:9–13 (NIV)

Focus Daily: "And when you pray, do not be like the hypocrites, for they love to pray standing in the synagogues and on the street corners to be seen by others. Truly I tell you, they have received their reward in full. But when you pray, go into your room, close the door and pray to your Father, who is unseen. Then your Father, who sees what is done in secret, will reward you." (Matthew 6:5–6 NIV)

Focus Questions: What problem regarding prayer is Jesus addressing in his culture? Do you see anything like this today? How do you personally respond?

Practice Daily: If you haven't already, identify a physical space that will be your prayer room for the next twelve weeks. Today, pray through each section of the Lord's Prayer through the framework of your family. Try to redirect your thoughts away from your immediate needs and pray through your family identity as a whole.

JOURNAL DAILY
(Write at least three sentences per day):

Jesus Prayed

MEMORIZE

This, then, is how you should pray:
"Our Father in heaven,
hallowed be your name,
your kingdom come,
your will be done,
on earth as it is in heaven.
Give us today our daily bread.
And forgive us our debts,
as we also have forgiven our debtors.
And lead us not into temptation,
but deliver us from the evil one."
—Matthew 6:9–13 (NIV)

Focus Daily: "And when you pray, do not keep on babbling like pagans, for they think they will be heard because of their many words. Do not be like them, for your Father knows what you need before you ask Him." (Matthew 6:7–8 NIV)

Focus Questions: What additional problem regarding prayer is Jesus addressing? Do you see anything like this today? If your Father already knows what you need before you ask, why should you ask anyway?

Practice Daily: Pray through each section of the Lord's Prayer through the framework of your community. It could be your church, your workplace, your team, or your club. This is a group you belong to that is outside of and larger than your immediate family. Try to focus your prayer time on this group as a whole.

JOURNAL DAILY
(Write at least three sentences per day):

Jesus Prayed

MEMORIZE

This, then, is how you should pray:
"Our Father in heaven,
hallowed be your name,
your kingdom come,
your will be done,
on earth as it is in heaven.
Give us today our daily bread.
And forgive us our debts,
as we also have forgiven our debtors.
And lead us not into temptation,
but deliver us from the evil one."
—Matthew 6:9–13 (NIV)

Focus Daily: "One of those days Jesus went out to a mountainside to pray, and spent the night praying to God. When morning came, He called his disciples to him and chose twelve of them, whom He also designated apostles." (Luke 6:12–13 NIV)

Focus Questions: Jesus prayed all night then chose the disciples. Why pray all night? Why couldn't he just choose them based on his own resources? What is our Hero modeling for us?

Practice Daily: Today pray through each section of the Lord's Prayer through the framework of your nation. It could be your city, state, or the country. See yourself as a part of this much greater whole. Observe how seeing the prayer through this lens changes it for you. Identify and pray for leaders by name including leaders with whom you may disagree.

JOURNAL DAILY
(Write at least three sentences per day):

_____

_____

_____

_____

_____

_____

_____

_____

_____

_____

_____

_____

_____

_____

_____

_____

Jesus Prayed

MEMORIZE

This, then, is how you should pray:
"Our Father in heaven,
hallowed be your name,
your kingdom come,
your will be done,
on earth as it is in heaven.
Give us today our daily bread.
And forgive us our debts,
as we also have forgiven our debtors.
And lead us not into temptation,
but deliver us from the evil one."
—Matthew 6:9–13 (NIV)

Focus Daily: "Then Jesus told his disciples a parable to show them that they should always pray and not give up. He said: 'In a certain town there was a judge who neither feared God nor cared what people thought. And there was a widow in that town who kept coming to him with the plea, "Grant me justice against my adversary."

For some time he refused. But finally he said to himself, 'Even though I don't fear God or care what people think, yet because this widow keeps bothering me, I will see that she gets justice, so that she won't eventually come and attack me!'"

And the Lord said, "Listen to what the unjust judge says. And will not God bring about justice for his chosen ones, who cry out to him day and night? Will he keep putting them off? I tell you, he will see that they get justice, and quickly." (Luke 18:1–8 NIV)

Focus Questions: Jesus taught His disciples to be diligent in prayer. How is Jesus encouraging us to approach God? How do you feel about it? Is this an easy or difficult instruction from our Hero?

Practice Daily: What is the life issue that has been with you the longest? Maybe it is one on which you have given up. It could be a burden for yourself, your health, finances, or a broken relationship. Revisit this in your prayer time today. Is it something you need to uphold and submit to God and His timing for a greater length of time? Be aware it could be weeks, months, or even years. Write it down below.

JOURNAL DAILY
(Write at least three sentences per day):

_____

_____

_____

_____

_____

_____

_____

_____

Jesus Prayed

MEMORIZE

This, then, is how you should pray:
"Our Father in heaven,
hallowed be your name,
your kingdom come,
your will be done,
on earth as it is in heaven.
Give us today our daily bread.
And forgive us our debts,
as we also have forgiven our debtors.
And lead us not into temptation,
but deliver us from the evil one."
—Matthew 6:9–13 (NIV)

Focus Daily: "Going a little farther, he fell with his face to the ground prayed, 'My Father, if it is possible, may this cup be taken from me. Yet not as I will, but as you will.'" (Matthew 26:39 NIV)

Focus Questions: In the Garden of Gethsemane, under unimaginable cosmic strain, Jesus asked His Father for another plan than the cross. Still, He went to Calvary. What was His posture as He approached the Father? What does that teach us about the way we ask of God?

Practice Daily: What are your greatest challenges and burdens? What requires your emotional energy right now? Bring those burdens before God with the image of Jesus before the Father in the Garden as a model for following Jesus in prayer.

JOURNAL DAILY

(Write at least three sentences per day):

_____

_____

_____

_____

_____

_____

_____

_____

_____

_____

_____

_____

_____

_____

Jesus Knew Scripture

The Bible is to me the most precious thing in the world just because it tells me the story of Jesus.
—George MacDonald

S cripture poured from Jesus. At nearly every turn, He used it to teach, encourage, and comfort those around Him. In the same way, He also depended on Scripture to explain and identify Himself, confound His adversaries, resist Satan's temptation, and even face death. Time and time again, Jesus exhibited both a passionate love for and an encyclopedic knowledge of the Old Testament.

As we follow in the footsteps of our Hero, we must love and embrace His word in both our coming and our going. His truth should be so deeply woven into our hearts that it spills into our prayer lives as well. It is through this practice that we are able to hear Him speak in and through us. Moreover, as we create space in the rhythm of our lives for relationship with God, we will be refined by the whisper of the Spirit and shaped by the shout of Scripture.

It is said that we know God by two revelations: the general revelation of nature and the special revelation of Scripture. In the same way, God has given us the personal revelation of Jesus. It is ultimately the job of the first two revelations to lead us to the last. In Jesus, we have the ultimate revelation of a God who would leave His heavenly privilege out of love just so we could know Him.

In John 5:39–40, Jesus told the religious leaders, "You study the Scriptures diligently because you think that in them you have eternal life. These are the very Scriptures that testify about me, yet you refuse to come to me to have life" (NIV).

The Bible is like gravity. It relentlessly and lovingly pulls us toward the Son who brings light and heat to it. It is why the study of Scripture apart from Jesus will leave us cold with legalism, discouragement, or, worse yet, arrogance. When we read Scripture, we must see that it always points beyond itself and has its fulfillment in Jesus: "[Jesus said,] 'Do not think that I have come to abolish the Law or the Prophets; I have not come to abolish them but to fulfill them'" (Matthew 5:17 NIV).

It is safe to say that Jesus didn't have a copy of the Scriptures that He carried around as He ministered to others. Scripture written on scrolls and parchment in the first century was extremely expensive and labor intensive to reproduce. Typically, only the local synagogue would have a copy of the Books of Moses, the Psalms, and the Prophets. It was a regular practice for the Scriptures to be read aloud during synagogue gatherings, but it was very unusual for individuals to have their own copy, something that was reserved for the rich.

Like any good Jewish boy, Jesus learned the Scriptures first from his parents and then his local rabbi. Typically, if a boy showed promise, he would be allowed to continue his education beyond the age of twelve. It was not unusual for children to have substantial portions of the Torah and Prophets committed to memory. And even though we don't have any record of how far Jesus's education went as a child, we do know he taught in the temple at the tender age of twelve, demonstrating a tremendous, authoritative grasp of the Scriptures.

Not until halfway through the festival did Jesus go up to the temple courts and begin to teach. The Jews there were amazed and asked, "How did this man get such learning without having been taught?" Jesus answered, "My teaching is not my own. It comes from the one who sent me. Anyone who chooses to do the will of God will find out whether my teaching comes from God or whether I speak on my own." (John 7:14–17 NIV)

When Jesus had finished saying these things, the crowds were amazed at his teaching, because he taught as one who had authority, and not as their teachers of the law. (Matthew 7:28–29 NIV)

The religious leaders were amazed at not only Jesus's grasp of Scripture, but at the authority with which He taught it. He exercised the right to reinterpret and challenge the traditional views held by the institutional leadership. Throughout the Sermon on the Mount, the longest recorded teaching from Jesus, we repeatedly see the phrase "you have heard it said, but I tell you." In each instance, Jesus was challenging and reframing a familiar Old Testament teaching. We see this clearly in Matthew 5:

You have heard that it was said to the people long ago, "You shall not murder, and anyone who murders will be subject to judgment." But I tell you that anyone who is angry with a brother or sister will be subject to judgment. (verses 21–22 NIV)

You have heard that it was said, "You shall not commit adultery." But I tell you that anyone who looks at a woman lustfully has already committed adultery with her in his heart. (verses 27–28 NIV)

You have heard that it was said, "Love your neighbor and hate your enemy." But I tell you, love your enemies and pray for those who persecute you, that you may be children of your Father in heaven. (verses 43–45 NIV)

But the most profound example of this in Scripture occurred when Jesus confronted the law of Moses in the story of the woman caught in adultery. Discovered in the act itself, this woman had been dragged up the temple steps in a ploy to expose Jesus as a false teacher. As she was forced into the temple courts, she would have been terrified. Because she knew, as everyone else knew, that adultery was punishable by death according to Old Testament law. She was brought before Jesus, screaming for her life and surrounded by a crowd. The Pharisees smugly looked on, believing they finally had Jesus cornered.

> They said to Jesus,] "Teacher, this woman was caught in the act of adultery. In the Law Moses commanded us to stone her. Now what do you say?" They were using this question as a trap, in order to have a basis for accusing him.
>
> But he bent down and started to write on the ground with his finger. When they kept on questioning him, he straightened up and said to them, "Let any one of you who is without sin be the first to throw a stone at her." Again he stooped down again and wrote on the ground.
>
> At this, those who heard began to go away one at a time, the older ones first, until only Jesus was left, with the woman still standing there. Jesus straightened up and asked her, "Woman, where are they? Has no one condemned you?"
>
> "No one, sir," she said.
>
> "Then neither do I condemn you," Jesus declared. "Go no and leave your life of sin." (John 8:4–11 NIV)

This is what it looks like when Jesus says, "I didn't come to abolish the law and the prophets but to fulfill them." Jesus brings life where there is death, mercy where there is judgment, and grace where there is condemnation.

As we read Scripture, whether the books of Moses or the letters of Paul, we must view it through the life and teaching of Jesus. He is the center point, the great unifying factor from which it is all to be understood and interpreted. We must always see the written word through the lens of the Living Word.

In order to do so we must be aware of the primary ways that we can learn Scripture: teaching, meditation, and memorization.

While these may seem self-explanatory, let's unpack the meaning of teaching and meditation as they relate to our journey. Teaching refers to the study of the Bible's entire narrative. This can be done through personal reading, public teaching, audiobooks, and any written work of great teachers and authors. Meditation is the practice of spending deliberate, focused time to contemplate specific passages of the Bible that are particularly meaningful to where we are in life.

It is important to remember that our goal is not to know more of the Bible than the next person. Our goal is to know the heart of God and to see more clearly our Hero's presence in all of Scripture. As we read, meditate, and memorize the Scripture, we should continue to ask ourselves, "Where is Jesus in this passage? How do we know God better? What is He saying to us?" We should spend some time there. We should linger in that moment and write down our thoughts. But keep in mind there may be days when we don't hear much of anything and other days when thoughts pour out of us. And that is truly okay. Like any relationship, we will experience a natural ebb and flow.

Last week, we began the weekly memorization of a short passage as it pertains to the week's practice. We will continue this throughout our twelve-week journey. We will spend some time this week meditating on and praying through various teachings in the Bible itself from our Hero and the New Testament writers.

Jesus Knew Scripture

MEMORIZE WEEKLY

Do not think that I have come to abolish
the Law or the Prophets; I have not come
to abolish them but to fulfill them.
—Matthew 5:17 (NIV)

Focus Daily: (Read the above verse.)

Focus Questions: What does this tell you about Jesus's relationship with the Old Testament? What does He mean by "fulfill"?

Practice Daily: Remember, as we begin, our posture in the practice is to create space for intimacy with God. Read Matthew 5:17–20. Sit and linger with that before you start. What is Jesus's attitude toward the Scripture here? Read the rest of the chapter and take note of places where Jesus says, "You have heard it said . . . but I tell you." How does that affect your view of Scripture? Pray over this for a few moments, and write your thoughts below.

JOURNAL DAILY

(Write at least three sentences per day):

_____

_____

_____

_____

_____

_____

_____

_____

_____

_____

_____

_____

_____

_____

_____

_____

_____

_____

Jesus Knew Scripture

MEMORIZE WEEKLY

Do not think that I have come to abolish
the Law or the Prophets; I have not come
to abolish them but to fulfill them.
—Matthew 5:17 (NIV)

Focus Daily: "You study the Scriptures diligently because you think that in them you have eternal life. These are the very Scriptures that testify about me, yet you refuse to come to me to have life" (John 5:39–40 NIV).

Focus Questions: What attitude about Scripture is Jesus addressing? Is He saying that respect for the Old Testament is a bad thing?

Practice Daily: Read John 5:37–47. Pray through this passage for a few minutes. What is God revealing to you about Jesus and Moses? What is He saying to you about Scripture? Throughout your day find three windows of time when you can read these few verses again. What sticks out to you the most?

JOURNAL DAILY

(Write at least three sentences per day):

_____

_____

_____

_____

_____

_____

_____

_____

_____

_____

_____

_____

_____

_____

_____

_____

_____

Jesus Knew Scripture

MEMORIZE WEEKLY

Do not think that I have come to abolish
the Law or the Prophets; I have not come
to abolish them but to fulfill them.
—Matthew 5:17 (NIV)

Focus Daily: "The tempter came to him and said, 'If you are the Son of God, tell these stones to become bread.' Jesus answered, 'It is written: "Man shall not live on bread alone, but on every word that comes from the mouth of God"'" (Matthew 4:3–4 NIV).

Focus Questions: What is Satan attempting to appeal to in Jesus's character? How does Jesus respond? What does He mean by "every word that comes from the mouth of God?"

Practice Daily: Today read and meditate on Matthew 4:1–11. What is the nature of each temptation? Why does Jesus respond the way He does? What is His example to us? How do we practically follow Him in this? Think through this today as you are challenged. How would you look to Scripture as a resource when you are tempted?

JOURNAL DAILY

(Write at least three sentences per day):

_____

_____

_____

_____

_____

_____

_____

_____

_____

_____

_____

_____

_____

_____

_____

_____

_____

Jesus Knew Scripture

MEMORIZE WEEKLY

Do not think that I have come to abolish
the Law or the Prophets; I have not come
to abolish them but to fulfill them.
—Matthew 5:17 (NIV)

Focus Daily: "For the word of God is alive and active. Sharper than any double-edged sword, it penetrates even to dividing soul and spirit, joints and marrow; it judges the thoughts and attitudes of the heart" (Hebrews 4:12 NIV).

Focus Questions: What characteristics does the author of Hebrews attribute to Scripture? How is it distinguished from other books? What has your experience been with Scripture?

Practice Daily: The author of Hebrews moves from passionately addressing God's rest for His people, to the living nature of Scripture as a living and active conduit, to this "rest relationship," and finally to speaking of Christ as the mediator for us, a high priest. He is someone who knows our struggles and temptations. Take some time to meditate on verses 14–16. Why does the author connect these thoughts of rest, Scripture, and Jesus as our priest? Pray and ask God what He would reveal to you through this passage. Make a point of revisiting this passage a few times throughout the day and see how it informs your attitude.

JOURNAL DAILY

(Write at least three sentences per day):

_____

_____

_____

_____

_____

_____

_____

_____

_____

_____

_____

_____

_____

_____

Jesus Knew Scripture

MEMORIZE WEEKLY

Do not think that I have come to abolish
the Law or the Prophets; I have not come
to abolish them but to fulfill them.
—Matthew 5:17 (NIV)

Focus Daily: "All Scripture is God-breathed and is useful for teaching, rebuking, correcting and training in righteousness, so that the servant of God may be thoroughly equipped for every good work" (2 Timothy 3:16–17 NIV).

Focus Questions: The apostle Paul encourages his student Timothy regarding Scripture in this passage. What is He saying about Scripture? What is he not saying? How is the phrase *so that* important here?

Practice Daily: In the same chapter read verses 1–7. Do you see any parallels today? Paul points to himself and to Scripture as examples of how to live in that world. Read the rest of the chapter and meditate on verse 15 for a few minutes. Revisit verse 15 at least three times during your day. What does "wise for salvation through faith in Christ Jesus" mean to you in your daily context?

JOURNAL DAILY

(Write at least three sentences per day):

Jesus Knew Scripture

MEMORIZE WEEKLY

*Do not think that I have come to abolish
the Law or the Prophets; I have not come
to abolish them but to fulfill them.*
—Matthew 5:17 (NIV)

Focus Daily: "What we have received is not the spirit of the world, but the Spirit who is from God, so that we may understand what God has freely given us. This is what we speak, not in words taught us by human wisdom but in words taught by the Spirit, explaining spiritual realities with Spirit-taught words" (1 Corinthians 2:12–13 NIV).

Focus Questions: In 1 Corinthians, Paul is writing to the church in Corinth, which was challenged by false teaching, sexual immorality, and divisions. What is he affirming in this passage? What is He affirming about Scripture?

Practice Daily: Read verses 6–16. Meditate on verse 16 for a few minutes. How do you have the "mind of Christ?" As you move through your day ask yourself, "What has the Spirit of God revealed to me that others might consider foolishness?"

JOURNAL DAILY

(Write at least three sentences per day):

_____

_____

_____

_____

_____

_____

_____

_____

_____

_____

_____

_____

_____

_____

_____

_____

Jesus Spent Time Alone

Solitude is the furnace of transformation.
—Henri Nouwen

O ur lives are so cluttered with noise and chatter. We crowd our hearts and minds with the constant drone of the world around us. Our brains get addicted to the never-ending stimulation and information washing over us at every turn, designed to tantalize and bait us to the next click. We are junkies to not only the noise, but also to the affirmation.

And while there are a hundred positive things about the information age, the downside is that the noise pushes out reflection. It confirms our natural biases, and it can numb us to our deepest fears. The more noise we surround ourselves with, the less likely we are to face ourselves honestly, and it turns us into reactive beings, always responding and rarely creating.

> ## "But Jesus often withdrew to lonely places and prayed."
>
> ### (Luke 5:16 NIV)

Imagine a world with no internet, no radio, no social media, no recorded music, no newspapers, no theaters, no television, no telephones, no texting, no binge-watching. This is how Jesus lived. But somehow even in an information-depleted world, He still found the need for silence and solitude. He found a way to create a natural rhythm that valued both His time with people and His time alone with His Father.

When preparing for the tests of leadership and public ministry, Jesus spent forty days alone in the desert (Matthew 4:1–11). Before choosing His twelve apostles, He spent the entire night alone in the desert (Luke 6:12–13). Upon receiving news of the death of John the Baptist, He withdrew in a boat to a solitary place (Matthew 14:13). After the miraculous feeding of the five thousand, Jesus retreated to the hills by Himself (Matthew 14:23).

It is clear that Jesus was comfortable taking time to be alone even when the demands on Him from others were great. If Jesus shows us what it looks like to "love the Lord your God with all your heart, soul, mind and strength" and to "love your neighbor as yourself," we should pay close attention to the rhythm he followed. Knowing that, Jesus spent time in silence and solitude as a way of creating more space for uninterrupted, concentrated time with his Father. If Jesus felt this was important, we most certainly need to prioritize it as well.

Solitude and community are complementary. One informs the other. Intimacy with God is necessary to love others well. And the love of others is necessary to love God well. When we separate one from the other, we get a false sense of religiosity. We either make an idol of human relationships leading to codependency and disappointment or we detach from others leading to a pious, self-centered, self-regarding faith not adequately grounded in love.

Dietrich Bonhoeffer put it like this: "Let him who cannot be alone beware of community. . . . Let him who is not in community beware of being alone. . . . Each by itself has profound perils and pitfalls. One who wants fellowship without solitude plunges into the void of words and feelings, and the one who seeks solitude without fellowship perishes in the abyss of vanity, self-infatuation and despair."*

---

* Dietrich Bonhoeffer, *Life Together* (New York: Harper & Row, 1954), 77.

We all have temperaments that lend themselves to one extreme or the other. For some, solitude is an easy practice to engage. And for others, it is uncomfortable, if not frightening. But do not see them as opposing forces. They are instead meant to complement each another. Jesus showed us that solitude isn't about being alone, but it is about spending time alone with God and cultivating a love relationship with His Son.

Imagine for a bit how exciting it would be to get time alone with one of our greatest earthly heroes. For the golf lover, it might be a few uninterrupted hours with Tiger Woods for a private lesson. For the music lover, it might be playing alongside The Edge of U2 for an afternoon while he shows you how he plays "Where the Streets Have No Name." Insert any interest or hero into this scenario, and we would clear the calendar, take time off from work, find someone to watch the kids, get up at the crack of dawn, and dip into our savings just to get those few precious hours with the someone we admire.

It is much the same when we find ourselves in love. We rearrange our lives to get that one-on-one time. Laughing together, learning together, experiencing life in the context of just "you and me" is a precious commodity. And we will go to great lengths to get that concentrated time to better know and walk with the one we love apart from the distraction of other people.

It is this intimate love relationship with Jesus that pours out of us into our relationship with others. It is the true engine of our faith. And it is why it is so crucial for us to learn how to withdraw for that sacred time set apart to be alone with Him.

Sometimes solitude terrifies us. We fear to look in the mirror and see that self beneath the image we work so hard to project. We can feel undone at that moment. And we often can't bear the weight of facing our broken selves. But Jesus meets us in the silence and embraces us where we are, warts and all. He wants to speak to us lovingly when we finally have ears to hear. He says, "My son, my daughter, you are more loved than you can imagine. I cherish our time together. Let me love you in this space. Let me hold you close and speak wisdom into your listening ear. Let us have this time alone together so that we will walk more closely throughout the rest of your day. I want to give you abundant life. So enter into these quiet moments, rest and listen, and then we can face the day together."

There may be times, even in solitude, when we don't seem to hear anything from God. He may even feel further away. But we must endeavor to keep going, keep showing up, and keep creating space for closeness with the Father. Many who came before have felt the same way and endured to the other side. Even Jesus experienced distance from the Father in the quiet moments of his greatest need. Just trust that even when it is darkest, morning is coming. Jesus proves that to us with an empty tomb.

As we engage in this practice, we will follow these guidelines:

- Bring only the Bible and this book.
- Leave any devices in another room.
- If using an electronic Bible, turn off all other notifications and applications.
- Pray through the daily practices on the following pages without distraction of any kind.

Know it will be uncomfortable at first. Quieting the noise in our heads takes some time. But it will be worth pushing through your discomfort as you set aside this sacred time with the Lover of your soul.

Jesus Spent Time Alone

MEMORIZE WEEKLY

But Jesus often withdrew to lonely places and prayed.
—Luke 5:16 (NIV)

Focus Daily: (Read the above verse.)

Focus Questions: How often is "often?" When Jesus, went away to pray was He lonely? Where is a solitary place for you to spend time with God?

Practice Daily: Remember, as we begin, our posture in the practice is to create space for intimacy with God. Regarding the above verse, "lonely" can be misleading. Other translations use the word *deserted* or *desolate*. Jesus withdrew to places where there were few people. But He was hardly alone. You have already identified your prayer closet in our first week. Look at the rest of your week and carve out a substantial window of time—a minimum of three hours—for you to truly be alone with God. Maybe an afternoon or morning of the upcoming weekend. Put this on your calendar as a nonnegotiable meeting with your Hero.

JOURNAL DAILY

(Write at least three sentences per day):

_____

_____

_____

_____

_____

_____

_____

_____

_____

_____

_____

_____

_____

_____

_____

_____

_____

_____

Jesus Spent Time Alone

But Jesus often withdrew to lonely places and prayed.
—Luke 5:16 (NIV)

Focus Daily: "Very early in the morning, while it was still dark, Jesus got up, left the house and went off to a solitary place, where he prayed" (Mark 1:35 NIV).

Focus Questions: Why do you suppose Jesus chose the very early morning to leave the house and go to a solitary place? How does that inform your own alone time with God?

Practice Daily: Everyone was looking for Jesus, but after His time in prayer He told His disciples that it was time for them to move on to another village. It appears in this instance that Jesus set off to be alone with His Father in order to make a decision as to where He and His disciples would go next. There will be a moment today when you will have a decision to make. It might be a small thing or a very significant thing. Before settling that decision, break away from the noise and find a few moments when you can be alone with God.

JOURNAL DAILY

(Write at least three sentences per day):

Jesus Spent Time Alone

MEMORIZE WEEKLY

But Jesus often withdrew to lonely places and prayed.
—Luke 5:16 (NIV)

Focus Daily: "When Jesus heard [that John the Baptist had been beheaded], he withdrew by boat privately to a solitary place" (Matthew 14:13 NIV).

Focus Questions: Jesus said, "Truly I tell you, among those born of women there has not risen anyone greater than John the Baptist" (Matthew 11:11 NIV). John was a prophet and the forerunner to Jesus's coming. Why do you think Jesus withdrew after John was martyred?

Practice Daily: When in your life have you suffered a recent loss? You may still feel the grief of it. You may have already processed it to a great degree. It could be a health challenge, a career disappointment, the loss of a loved one, or any number of things great or small. Today as you withdraw to be with God, bring that loss to Him. Ask Him to bring healing and resolve in your heart. Ask Him to bear the burden with you.

JOURNAL DAILY

(Write at least three sentences per day):

_____

_____

_____

_____

_____

_____

_____

_____

_____

_____

_____

_____

_____

_____

_____

_____

_____

_____

Jesus Spent Time Alone

MEMORIZE WEEKLY

But Jesus often withdrew to lonely places and prayed.
—Luke 5:16 (NIV)

Focus Daily: "After [Jesus] had dismissed [the crowds], he went up on a mountainside by himself to pray. Later that night, he was [still] there alone" (Matthew 14:23 NIV).

Focus Questions: We know that there were many reasons why Jesus would want to withdraw and be alone with the Father. In this scenario, what could be His motivations?

Practice Daily: What is the situation in your regular life rhythm, whether daily, weekly or monthly, that truly drains you of energy? Today identify that situation and come up with a plan to be alone with God in order to recharge in the aftermath.

JOURNAL DAILY

(Write at least three sentences per day):

_____

_____

_____

_____

_____

_____

_____

_____

_____

_____

_____

_____

_____

_____

_____

_____

_____

Jesus Spent Time Alone

MEMORIZE WEEKLY

But Jesus often withdrew to lonely places and prayed.
—Luke 5:16 (NIV)

Focus Daily: "After his brothers had gone up to the feast, then [Jesus] also went up, not publicly but in private" (John 7:10 ESV).

Focus Questions: Jesus decided to be alone for a significant amount of time before attending what amounted to a large celebration. We can't really know His mind in this, but why do you think He made this choice?

Practice Daily: In the above scenario, Jesus walked 90 miles from Galilee to Jerusalem, which gave him about five days of solitude. For us, that would be a lot of drive time. But travel time can be invaluable because it takes us away from our normal rhythms. Whether it is the drive to work or school or a more significant flight, approach that time this week as an opportunity to be alone with God. It might be five minutes or five hours. Turn off the radio, podcasts, audiobooks, and news channel, and use that time to let your mind be still and listen for the "still, small voice" of God.

JOURNAL DAILY

(Write at least three sentences per day):

_____

_____

_____

_____

_____

_____

_____

_____

_____

_____

_____

_____

_____

_____

_____

_____

_____

_____

_____

Jesus Spent Time Alone

MEMORIZE WEEKLY

But Jesus often withdrew to lonely places and prayed.
—Luke 5:16 (NIV)

Focus Daily: "Again [the religious leaders in Jerusalem] sought to arrest [Jesus], but he escaped from their hands. He went away again [walking about five miles] across the Jordan to the place where John had been baptizing at first, and there he remained. And many came to him" (John 10:39–41 ESV).

Focus Questions: Jesus retreated to a place that would have had great spiritual significance for Him. Why do you think He would revisit this place when He was under stress?

Practice Daily: Is there a physical landmark in your life that has great spiritual significance or symbolism to you? Identify that and write the story behind it in your journal entry below. If possible, make a plan to visit that place and get some alone time with the Father.

JOURNAL DAILY

(Write at least three sentences per day):

_____

_____

_____

_____

_____

_____

_____

_____

_____

_____

_____

_____

_____

_____

_____

_____

_____

_____

Jesus Slowed Down

In our rushing, bulls in china shops, we break our own lives.
—Ann Voskamp

We live in an era of fast. Fast food, fast cars, fast internet speed, fast-track careers, fast delivery, fast dating, fast relationship starts, and fast relationship stops. As a culture, we are obsessed with speed.

One-click ordering with two-day delivery. Order your food on an app so it is ready at the restaurant counter when you arrive. We text instead of call because calling takes too much time. Why converse when one sentence will do? We have even reduced our text messages to abbreviated words and acronyms. We text "Thx" because "thanks" is three letters too many to express our gratitude. LOL!

News gets delivered to us so quickly from so many sources we no longer know who to believe and what actually happened. We want things as quickly as possible for fear of missing out or fear of being passed by. We listen to our podcasts and audiobooks at double speed because there is just too much we need to know and not enough time. Perhaps we think if we don't keep up we will be obsolete before the day is done. And no one wants to be "that guy."

But we are exhausted. We are soul weary when all this speed and efficiency was supposed to make our lives better. Instead, we are more stressed and more fearful, and have more superficial short-term relationships than we ever imagined. The definition of "friend" has taken on a whole new, much smaller, meaning than ever before.

To be fair, the efficiency and speed of technology in our society have many helpful aspects. Modern medicine, communication, and education in the West have made it possible to live longer, healthier lives than at any other time in human history. The challenge for us is to learn how to discern and filter the information and services available to us. Wisdom must prevail over information for us to live in the richness and abundance of life that God intends for his children. As always, we look to our Hero as the timeless model for our lives.

Jesus was never in a hurry but also didn't hesitate to move forward if His Kingdom required it. We see Him continually urged by the people around Him to move it along. We find Him lingering where He should have left. And we find Him moving on when those around Him begged Him to stay.

Even in the bigger story of God's relationship with humanity, He exhibits tremendous patience. Peter reminds us, "But do not forget this one thing, dear friends: With the Lord a day is like a thousand years, and a thousand years are like a day. The Lord is not slow in keeping his promise, as some understand slowness" (2 Peter 3:8–9 NIV). God, through Jesus, has His own time and purpose for everything. After the Old Testament writers finished, Israel was silent for 400 years—no more prophets or poets in that time.

But when the fullness of time had come, God sent forth his Son.

(Galatians 4:4 ESV)

Jesus showed up on the scene when the timing was right. He even waited until He was thirty years old to begin His public ministry. Why not twenty-five? Why not twenty? In our minds, we might think, "Surely, he could've accomplished so much more had he started earlier!" But Jesus honored His Father's perfect timing. Even as He prepared for the first miraculous sign of His ministry when He would turn water into wine, He acknowledged, "My hour has not yet come."

Perhaps the most extraordinary example of this is when Jesus was told His very dear friend, Lazarus, was sick to the point of death. On receiving this news, Jesus waited. His followers were undoubtedly confused by the delay. They all knew how close He was to the young man, how much He loved him, and how easily He could have healed him as He had healed so many others. But Jesus arrived after Lazarus had been dead for four days. It was then, to the glory of His Father and a testimony to who He is, that Jesus raised Lazarus to life.

It is important to note that slowing down doesn't mean that you suddenly become unproductive. Counterintuitively, studies show us that hurried people aren't any more productive than unhurried people, yet they experience significantly more stress. Our culture very frequently rewards the overly busily, overly hurried type-A personalities. And when someone asks you how you are doing it is both a complaint and a badge of honor to say, "I'm so busy!" The research shows us that busyness is not just the enemy of life satisfaction, but it severely inhibits intimacy with our significant others. This has become so prevalent in our culture that psychologists have come up with a clinical term to describe it: "hurry sickness."

If you think this may be an issue for you, here are some symptoms as described by authors Rosemary K. M. Sword and Philip Zimbardo, PhD, in *Psychology Today*:

- Moving from one check-out line to another because it looks shorter/faster.
- Counting the cars in front of you and either getting in the lane that has the least or is going the fastest.
- Multi-tasking to the point of forgetting one of the tasks.
- Accidentally putting your clothes on inside-out or backwards.

- Sleeping in your daytime clothes to save time in the morning.*

We all exhibit similar symptoms at one time or another. And the data is in. We all benefit from slowing down and creating more space with less stress for ourselves in both the workplace and our personal lives.

But is slowing down a kind of laziness? On the contrary, when we slow down with the kind of intentionality that Jesus exhibited, it can be harder. When we are moving quickly, momentum carries us along from one task to the next task, one location to the next location, crowding out our capacity to be interrupted. We can be in such a rush that we miss the divine appointments God would have for us. To slow down, in this regard, can take a disproportionate amount of energy. But as we follow our Hero, we will make room for the best things while sacrificing the busyness of the good or even acceptable things.

Author Dallas Willard was known for operating on "Dallas time." He never seemed to be in a rush. At the same time, he produced an enormously influential body of work. He was once asked what one needs to do for a spiritually healthy life. Dallas answered, "You must ruthlessly eliminate hurry from your life."

"OK, great! I'll write that down," said the questioner. "What else?"

"There is nothing else. You must ruthlessly eliminate hurry from your life."

Here is a world-famous author, teacher, speaker, and spiritual authority, renowned for his insight and wisdom and sought out by leaders from every corner of the globe. He has authored some of the greatest books on Christianity in the last century. This is a man who chaired the department of philosophy at USC. And yet this is his advice for a spiritually healthy life.

In three years, Jesus accomplished more in human history than anyone could have imagined. But Jesus also continually and repeatedly

---

* Rosemary K. M. Sword and Philip Zimbardo, "Hurry Sickness: Is the Quest to Do All and Be All Costing Us Our Health?," *Psychology Today*, February 9, 2013, https://www.psychologytoday.com/us/blog/the-time-cure/201302/hurry-sickness.

slowed down. Jesus slowed down for children. Jesus slowed down for women. Jesus slowed down for a hated tax collector. Jesus slowed down for a prostitute. Jesus slowed down for a Roman centurion, a sick Gentile, and for "that girl" with a questionable reputation.

Slowing down allows us to see more clearly. It allows us to see people God has placed in our path. It allows us to see the beauty all around us. It allows us to see God's hand at work and the opportunities, interactions, and intricacies of life He has gifted us.

As we discussed in previous chapters, Jesus had a life rhythm that created space for intimacy with God and with people. He showed us what it's like to love the Lord with all our hearts, souls, minds, and strength and to love our neighbors as ourselves. It simply cannot be done in a hurry. If we are to follow Jesus as our Hero, we can't follow him by running ahead. Abundant life in Christ always comes slowly—because love always takes time.

Jesus Slowed Down

MEMORIZE WEEKLY

Love is patient.
—1 Corinthians 13:4 (NIV)

Focus Daily: (Read the above verse.)

Focus Questions: When we see this verse we tend to think of it as being patient with the shortcomings of the one loved. And that is certainly a component of its meaning. But what if you read it as "love isn't in a hurry?"

Practice Daily: Remember, as always, our posture in these practices is to create space for intimacy with God and intimacy with other people. The clutter and hurry of life are truly the enemy of intimacy with both God and people. Make an effort today to listen to those closest to you more slowly. That is, listen without formulating your response and without rushing to resolution. Take more time than usual to answer their questions without agitation or impatience as you consciously ask the Spirit for loving guidance. Purosefully priortize the people who are present versus the people on the other end of your smart phone.

JOURNAL DAILY

(Write at least three sentences per day):

_____

_____

_____

_____

_____

_____

_____

_____

_____

_____

_____

_____

_____

_____

_____

_____

_____

_____

Jesus Slowed Down

MEMORIZE WEEKLY

Love is patient.
—1 Corinthians 13:4 (NIV)

Focus Daily: "When a Samaritan woman came to draw water, Jesus said to her, 'Will you give me a drink?' (His disciples had gone into the town to buy food.) The Samaritan woman said to him, 'You are a Jew and I am a Samaritan woman. How can you ask me for a drink?' (For Jews do not associate with Samaritans.)" (John 4:7–9 NIV).

Focus Questions: In this culture a Jew would have nothing to do with a Samaritan, and a man would not feel free to speak with a woman. In addition, this woman had a checkered reputation with a number of failed marriages and moral compromise. But Jesus lingered and took the time to see this woman and meet her in her story. Who is the person or group of people in your circle of influence who are the wrong type of people for you to interact with?

Practice Daily: We are going to learn to slow down both internally and externally. Today walk slowly around your home, your office, your neighborhood, or wherever it is you're going. Literally slow down your pace. Make it a point to observe and possibly make eye contact with the people along your path.

JOURNAL DAILY

(Write at least three sentences per day):

Jesus Slowed Down

MEMORIZE WEEKLY

Love is patient.
—1 Corinthians 13:4 (NIV)

Focus Daily: "But Martha was distracted by all the preparations that had to be made. She came to him and asked, 'Lord, don't you care that my sister has left me to do the work by myself? Tell her to help me!'

'Martha, Martha,' the Lord answered, 'you are worried and upset about many things, but few things are needed—or indeed only one. Mary has chosen what is better, and it will not be taken away from her'" (Luke 10:40–42 NIV).

Focus Questions: What good things do you find yourself busy with that are crowding out the best things?

Practice Daily: Make a list of those great things you have in your mind to do but simply don't have the time to do them. They could be spiritual practices, they could be relationships, or they could be as simple as maintaining your health.

JOURNAL DAILY

(Write at least three sentences per day):

Jesus Slowed Down

MEMORIZE WEEKLY

Love is patient.
—1 Corinthians 13:4 (NIV)

Focus Daily: "Then people brought little children to Jesus for him to place his hands on them and pray for them. But the disciples rebuked them.

Jesus said, 'Let the little children come to me, and do not hinder them, for the kingdom of heaven belongs to such as these'" (Matthew 19:13–14 NIV).

Focus Questions: Children held a very low place in this culture. Even Jesus disciples's thought children were a waste of time. Why do you think Jesus prioritized and took time with children?

Practice Daily: Take your list from yesterday and prioritize the items on it by number. Strategize on ways to slow down your life rhythm in order to pursue the top three items.

JOURNAL DAILY

(Write at least three sentences per day):

_____

_____

_____

_____

_____

_____

_____

_____

_____

_____

_____

_____

_____

_____

_____

_____

_____

_____

Jesus Slowed Down

MEMORIZE WEEKLY

Love is patient.
—1 Corinthians 13:4 (NIV)

Focus Daily: "Jesus entered Jericho and was passing through. A man was there by the name of Zacchaeus; he was a chief tax collector and was wealthy. He wanted to see who Jesus was, but because he was short he could not see over the crowd. So he ran ahead and climbed a sycamore-fig tree to see Him, since Jesus was coming that way.

When Jesus reached the spot, He looked up and said to him, 'Zacchaeus, come down immediately. I must stay at your house today.' So he came down at once and welcomed Him gladly" (Luke 19:1–6 NIV).

Focus Questions: Jesus was on his way somewhere else with the crowds pressing on him from every side. But he stopped for this man who would've been hated by other Jews. Why was it important for Jesus to slow down for this man?

Practice Daily: We can be in such a rush that we often miss the beauty around us. Three times today stop and focus on something truly beautiful. It could be the sky, children at the playground, or a great piece of art. Deliberately stop yourself and fix your eyes on it for at least fifteen seconds. It doesn't sound like much, but studies show it takes us at least that much time to truly see something

JOURNAL DAILY

(Write at least three sentences per day):

_____

_____

_____

_____

_____

_____

_____

_____

_____

_____

_____

_____

_____

_____

_____

_____

_____

Jesus Slowed Down

MEMORIZE WEEKLY

Love is patient.
—1 Corinthians 13:4 (NIV)

Focus Daily: "So the sisters sent word to Jesus, 'Lord, the one you love is sick.'

When he heard this, Jesus said, 'This sickness will not end in death. No, it is for God's glory so that God's Son may be glorified through it.' Now Jesus loved Martha and her sister and Lazarus. So when he heard that Lazarus was sick, he stayed where he was two more days" (John 11:3–6 NIV).

Focus Questions: Jesus deliberately waited until Lazarus has been dead for four days. People in this culture were superstitious that the spirit of a person lingered over the body for three days after death. Why did Jesus show up when he did?

Practice Daily: Make a point today to drive more slowly. Stay in the slow lane. When you go to the store, pick the longest line. Where there's an opportunity for someone else to go in front of you, let him or her. Make every effort to move a little more slowly throughout the day wherever you are. Pray and ask God to show you where He is at work all around you.

JOURNAL DAILY

(Write at least three sentences per day):

_____

_____

_____

_____

_____

_____

_____

_____

_____

_____

_____

_____

_____

_____

_____

_____

_____

Jesus Fasted

Fasting confirms our utter dependence upon God by finding in Him a source of sustenance beyond food.
—Dallas Willard

While it was quite commonplace in our Hero's lifetime, fasting gets a bad rap these days. Many see it through a legalistic framework, believing we don't need to prove our commitment to God by denying ourselves food. After all, we live in an age of freedom and grace. Moreover, there is no explicit biblical command for Christ-followers to fast. Jesus never came out and said, "You must fast for me to be pleased with you."

All of that is true.

And yet, Jesus fasted for forty days before beginning His public ministry. On some occasions, He even talked about fasting with His disciples as if it was assumed they were going to follow suit, an assumption that became even more apparent when He gave them guidelines as to how fasting aligned with the purpose of His Kingdom.

We don't need to deny ourselves food to please God. We aren't earning brownie points by punishing ourselves. When we think of fasting, we often see all the negative examples of overly pious, legalistic, religious folk who use it as a way to elevate themselves over others. Not a very appealing practice from that perspective.

It is interesting, however, that we see Jesus fasted for forty days before beginning his public ministry. When tempted by Satan in the wilderness, Jesus responded with Scripture in the midst of His hunger, declaring His dependence on God for life rather than just physical food.

> "Man shall not live on bread alone, but on every word that comes from the mouth of God."

(Matthew 4:4 NIV)

In the same way, we can fast to remind ourselves that God provides everything that we need, be it the breath in our lungs or the sight to our eyes: "Every good and perfect gift is from above, coming down from the Father of the heavenly lights, who does not change like shifting shadows" (James 1:17 NIV). In fasting, hunger pings our soul and prompts us to remember that light and life come from God, just as it also allows that hunger to shape our thoughts and spark gratitude toward the Father, who is our ultimate sustenance and joy.

Consider Jesus's instruction to His disciples in Matthew 6: "And when you fast, do not look gloomy like the hypocrites, for they disfigure their faces that their fasting may be seen by others. Truly, I say to you, they have received their reward. But when you fast, anoint your head and wash your face, that your fasting may not be seen by others but by your Father who is in secret. And your Father who sees in secret will reward you" (Matthew 6:16–18 ESV).

His instruction points to the truth that fasting is intensely personal. It is between you and God alone. It is sacred, focusing the heart and mind in the direction of our Creator. It is meant to carve out space in our lives (and in our bodies) to cultivate greater intimacy and dependence on God.

Jesus also tells us that the most significant benefit we get from the experience is lost if we practice it to gain attention from others: "Then John's disciples came and asked [Jesus], 'How is it that we and the

Pharisees fast often, but your disciples do not fast?' Jesus answered, 'How can the guests of the bridegroom mourn while he is with them? The time will come when the bridegroom will be taken from them; then they will fast" (Matthew 9:14–15 NIV).

This scenario can be looked at in a number of ways. Jesus was instructing John's disciples on the priority of fasting. This instruction may have come as a rebuke to the disciples' misplaced interest in fasting as a way to demonstrate their piety. On the other hand, it may have also come as a response to their jealousy that Jesus's disciples didn't fast as frequently as they did. Maybe they were just jealous. "How come we have to go hungry, and they don't?" This sounds a little like something you would hear on a sixth-grade playground. (Kidding . . . a little.) But regardless of the motive, His instruction serves the purpose of inclining our hearts toward the promise of His return. Because just as our hunger reminds us that our security isn't in our present circumstance, it also points us toward Jesus as our hope and our future, and as His followers, our stories become a part of His greater Kingdom story.

Here we have an example from the book of Acts:

"While they were worshiping the Lord and fasting, the Holy Spirit said, 'Set apart for me Barnabas and Saul for the work to which I have called them.' So after they had fasted and prayed, they placed their hands on them and sent them off." (Acts 13:2–3 NIV)

As you can see, the early church clearly had a practice of prayer and fasting. They fasted and prayed when vital decisions or issues were to be considered. They fasted and prayed when they were challenged and under persecution. They fasted and prayed in celebration and worship. For millennia, it has been a practice of Christ followers to use fasting as a way of focusing the heart in prayer over urgent issues and decisions. And for us today, the same is true. When we are faced with life's challenges, we can use this practice like Jesus and His followers did to focus our energy on the issue at hand. As the body reminds us that there is a need to address, we can redirect that energy toward trusting Him with our request.

It is interesting to note that nearly every culture and religious tradition in the world practices fasting. Much more can be said about the discipline of the body in this regard. Many who regularly practice fasting see it as a way of mastering their own physical desires. The assumption is that if one can be disciplined in this kind of abstinence, the benefit will flow over to many other areas of life. Jesus's disciples would have inherited this mindset from the Old Testament tradition, and there is a tremendous value to viewing it this way. Jesus reframed and realigned the practice toward a healthier, less legalistic, and more sustainable way of uniting our physicality and our spirituality. He reminded us that those two worlds overlap far more than we realize.

In our own modern version of fasting, we often abstain from things like social media, caffeine, alcohol, television, movies, and a variety of other items. And it can be beneficial to refrain from any number of these things, we should follow in the footsteps of our Hero and fast as He fasted. We all may find ourselves coming up against any number of our own protests: "I can't possibly go without food for a day. I will get cranky. I will get a headache. I will become less productive. Surely, God doesn't want me to experience any of that, does He?"

But in our obedience, God will make a way. Remember, millions have gone before you and practiced this kind of fast. Christ followers have been doing this for a very long time and have found tremendous benefit. So in preparation, let us pray that He will reveal an aspect of our lives or circumstance that needs focused attention and prayer. We will then pick a day to fast and offer up our concerns to God. It may focus on a need or a habit to break, or it may just be a time to refocus our hearts toward Jesus as our sustainer. But no matter how it unfolds, it will be an experience to remember and a practice to repeat periodically on our spiritual journey with Him.

Jesus Fasted

MEMORIZE WEEKLY

After fasting forty days and forty nights, he was hungry. The tempter came to him and said, "If you are the Son of God, tell these stones to become bread."

Jesus answered, "It is written: 'Man shall not live on bread alone, but on every word that comes from the mouth of God.'"
—Matthew 4:2–4 (NIV)

Focus Daily: (Read the above verse.)

Focus Questions: Jesus retreated to the wilderness and fasted for a very long time. When tempted with food in His extreme hunger, why did Jesus respond with this particular verse?

Practice Daily: Remember, as always, our posture in these practices is to create space for intimacy with God and with other people. This week we are going to exercise two different kinds of fasting. As you read in the previous chapter, our primary focus will be a fast from food. Pick a day this week that you'll abstain from food from sunrise to sunset. Put it on the calendar, and set yourself a reminder.

JOURNAL DAILY

(Write at least three sentences per day):

DAY 2

Jesus Fasted

MEMORIZE WEEKLY

After fasting forty days and forty nights, he was hungry. The tempter came to him and said, "If you are the Son of God, tell these stones to become bread."

Jesus answered, "It is written: 'Man shall not live on bread alone, but on every word that comes from the mouth of God.'"
—Matthew 4:2–4 (NIV)

Focus Daily: "Then John's disciples came and asked [Jesus], 'How is it that we and the Pharisees fast often, but your disciples do not fast?' Jesus answered, 'How can the guests of the bridegroom mourn while he is with them? The time will come when the bridegroom will be taken from them; then they will fast" (Matthew 9:14–15 NIV).

Focus Questions: Jesus was instructing John the Baptist's disciples when they inquired about fasting. As you look toward fasting, how could that time when the hunger gradually rises up in you over the course of the day point you toward your hope in Christ?

Practice Daily: We are going to practice a second kind of fast this week that is not food related. What has a constant presence in your life? Is it social media or the news or entertainment of some kind? Do you have some other habit? Today, identify that item and pick a day this week (apart from your fasting day) when you will abstain from it.

JOURNAL DAILY
(Write at least three sentences per day):

Jesus Fasted

MEMORIZE WEEKLY

After fasting forty days and forty nights, he was
hungry. The tempter came to him and said, "If you are
the Son of God, tell these stones to become bread."

Jesus answered, "It is written: 'Man shall
not live on bread alone, but on every word
that comes from the mouth of God.'"
—Matthew 4:2–4 (NIV)

Focus Daily: "And when you fast, do not look gloomy like the hypocrites,
for they disfigure their faces that their fasting may be seen by others.
Truly, I say to you, they have received their reward. But when you fast,
anoint your head and wash your face, that your fasting may not be seen
by others but by your Father who is in secret. And your Father who sees
in secret will reward you" (Matthew 6:16–18 ESV).

Focus Questions: Why would someone want to make it apparent to
other people that he or she is fasting? What do you think "your father
who sees in secret will reward you" means?

Practice Daily: Remind yourself today that the fast is not a way to gain
God's favor. You already have His favor and extravagant love. The fast
is another way to lean in and focus your heart on your relationship with
Him and to lift up an area of concern to Him.

JOURNAL DAILY

(Write at least three sentences per day):

Jesus Fasted

MEMORIZE WEEKLY

After fasting forty days and forty nights, he was
hungry. The tempter came to him and said, "If you are
the Son of God, tell these stones to become bread."

Jesus answered, "It is written: 'Man shall
not live on bread alone, but on every word
that comes from the mouth of God.'"
—Matthew 4:2–4 (NIV)

Focus Daily: "While they were worshiping the Lord and fasting, the Holy
Spirit said, 'Set apart for me Barnabas and Saul for the work to which I
have called them.' So after they had fasted and prayed, they placed their
hands on them and sent them off" (Acts 13:2–3 NIV).

Focus Questions: How can you see fasting within the framework
of worship? Have you ever thought of fasting and prayer as a way of
supporting someone you love for a purpose?

Practice Daily: In your journal entry today write down the name of a
friend or relative who has a significant challenge in front of him or her.
Write down what that challenge is, and pick a time over the next few
weeks when you will pray and fast for their concern.

JOURNAL DAILY

(Write at least three sentences per day):

Jesus Fasted

MEMORIZE WEEKLY

After fasting forty days and forty nights, he was hungry. The tempter came to him and said, "If you are the Son of God, tell these stones to become bread."

Jesus answered, "It is written: 'Man shall not live on bread alone, but on every word that comes from the mouth of God.'"
—Matthew 4:2–4 (NIV)

Focus Daily: "And Jesus rebuked the demon, and it came out of him, and the boy was healed that very hour. Then the disciples came to Jesus privately and asked, 'Why couldn't we drive it out?' He told them, 'Because of your lack of faith. I tell all of you with certainty, if you have faith like a grain of mustard seed, you can say to this mountain, "Move from here to there," and it will move; and nothing will be impossible for you.' But this kind does not come out except by prayer and fasting" (Matthew 17:18–21 ISV).

Focus Questions: The disciples were confronted with a demon-possessed boy whom they could not help. Why would Jesus follow up a comment on faith with a statement about prayer and fasting?

Practice Daily: If you haven't already done one of your two fasts this week, pick one for today and the other for tomorrow. Dedicate this time to walk more closely with Jesus throughout the day as the absence of food reminds us of our need for Him.

JOURNAL DAILY

(Write at least three sentences per day):

_____

_____

_____

_____

_____

_____

_____

_____

_____

_____

_____

_____

_____

_____

_____

_____

Jesus Fasted

MEMORIZE WEEKLY

After fasting forty days and forty nights, he was hungry. The tempter came to him and said, "If you are the Son of God, tell these stones to become bread."

Jesus answered, "It is written: 'Man shall not live on bread alone, but on every word that comes from the mouth of God.'"
—Matthew 4:2–4 (NIV)

Focus Daily: "Blessed are those who hunger and thirst for righteousness, for they shall be satisfied" (Matthew 5:6 NASB).

Focus Questions: What is righteousness in this context? How is it satisfied?

Practice Daily: In the ancient near East, food wasn't nearly as accessible as it is today in the West. Very few of us know what it is like to be truly hungry. When you fast this week, see if you can equate that physical hunger with what Jesus was referring to in Matthew 5:6. In your journal today, write down what it might take for you to be hungry for right standing with God. What need, as a person made in the image of God, can only be satisfied by God? Write down anything else God has revealed to you during your fasts.

JOURNAL DAILY

(Write at least three sentences per day):

Jesus Served

We should guard against the idea that worship is confined to the realm of thought, for Scripture links worship with service. During the temptation in the wilderness, our Lord quoted the Old Testament: 'You shall worship the Lord your God, and serve Him only' (Matt 4:10 cf. Deut 6:13, marg.). We should not separate what God has joined. Worship is no substitute for service, nor is service a substitute for worship. True worship will inevitably find expression in loving, sacrificial service
—Oswald Chambers

When Jesus was tempted by Satan, something profound happened. As Jesus weakened in body, Satan hoped Jesus would weaken in spirit as well. So Satan began the ultimate head game. His temptation started with asking Jesus to use His power to feed Himself. It was followed by Satan's request that Jesus prove His authority by throwing His body to destruction and having angelic minions save Him. And then came an enticing offer, one where Satan promised to grant Jesus all the kingdoms of the earth if He would only worship him for a moment. (See Matthew 4:8-11.) In each of these scenarios, Satan tempted Jesus to use His power to serve Himself. But at each turn, Jesus refused.

The most natural thing in the world for us is to use whatever power we have to serve ourselves and our little kingdoms. No one begrudges anyone using their status, their power, their finances, and so on to make their own lives a bit better. There's nothing wrong with that. But more often than not we do it with little to no consideration of anyone else, giving in to the old cliché, "You gotta look out for number 1." That is how the kingdoms of the world work. But the Kingdom of God is upside down. To find life, we must lose it. To gain real significance, we must embrace humility. To be great, we must become servants to everyone else.

In Matthew 20:20–28, we see a fascinating interaction between Jesus and the mother of two of His disciples:

> Then the mother of Zebedee's sons came to Jesus with her sons and, kneeling down, asked a favor of him.
>
> "What is it you want?" he asked.
>
> She said, "Grant that one of these two sons of mine may sit at your right and the other at your left in your kingdom."
>
> "You don't know what you are asking," Jesus said to them. "Can you drink the cup I am going to drink?"
>
> "We can," they answered.
>
> Jesus said to them, "You will indeed drink from my cup, but to sit at my right or left is not for me to grant. These places belong to those for whom they have been prepared by my Father."
>
> When the ten heard about this, they were indignant with the two brothers. Jesus called them together and said, "You know that the rulers of the Gentiles lord it over them, and their high officials exercise authority over them. Not so with you. Instead, whoever wants to become great among you must be your servant, and whoever wants to be first must be your slave—just as the Son of Man did not come to be served, but to serve, and to give his life as a ransom for many." (NIV)

Just like the ten, we may find ourselves wondering, "How on earth does this mama have the gall to approach Jesus with this kind of question?" But at the time, power and authority determined not only quality of life but also longevity. So she requested favor, the only thing that would allow her two sons and their future families to rise above Roman oppression and have a better life than she had known. Understanding this context, Jesus used her question as an opportunity to teach everyone about the nature of the Kingdom and how it would indeed rise above and beyond the Roman Empire, just as He was able to describe an upside-down Kingdom for his disciples and remind them that the one who serves most generously is who will gain the most authority.

Not only did Jesus surrender His right to use His power to serve Himself, but He also refused to use it in His defense. When asked to defend Himself and save His own life, He stood silently before Pilate, only to later articulate, "You would have no power over me if it were not given to you from above" (John 19:11 NIV). Even as He hanged dying on the Cross, people shouted that as a healer He should heal himself and come down. But Jesus refused to use His power to serve Himself. Instead, he offered forgiveness to those who scoffed at Him. He served others rather than himself in every conceivable way.

Throughout the Gospels, Jesus offered Himself generously. He use his power to heal, to teach, to challenge, and to encourage others without self-regard or expectation. He never bartered in an "if you do this for me, then I'll do this for you" exchange. His power was instead always used for the benefit of the other person. In this, our Hero modeled what it looks like to "love the Lord your God with all your heart, soul, and mind, and to love your neighbor as yourself."

Even before his crucifixion, Jesus gathered with his disciples to celebrate Passover and reframe what it meant to follow him, and in doing so He modeled His upside-down Kingdom once again.

Jesus knew that the Father had put all things under his power, and that he had come from God and was returning to God; so he got up from the meal, took off his outer clothing, and wrapped a towel around his waist. After that, he poured water into a basin and began to wash his disciples' feet, drying them with the towel that was wrapped around him.

He came to Simon Peter, who said to him, "Lord, are you going to wash my feet?"

Jesus replied, "You do not realize now what I am doing, but later you will understand."

"No," said Peter, "you shall never wash my feet."

Jesus answered, "Unless I wash you, you have no part with me."

"Then, Lord," Simon Peter replied, "not just my feet but my hands and my head as well!"

Jesus answered, "Those who have had a bath need only to wash their feet; their whole body is clean. And you are clean, though not every one of you." For he knew who was going to betray him, and that was why he said not everyone was clean.

When he had finished washing their feet, he put on his clothes and returned to his place. "Do you understand what I have done for you?" he asked them. "You call me 'Teacher' and 'Lord,' and rightly so, for that is what I am. Now that I, your Lord and Teacher, have washed your feet, you also should wash one another's feet. I have set you an example that you should do as I have done for you. Very truly I tell you, no servant is greater than his master, nor is a messenger greater than the one who sent him. Now that you know these things, you will be blessed if you do them." (John 13:3–17 NIV)

It's as though He is saying to us even now, "Please don't miss this. Remember this for the rest of your lives. And then tell everyone else to do likewise. My Kingdom doesn't operate the way the kingdoms of this world work because my Kingdom is not of this world. And neither are you if you follow after me. So, live in humility. Live in generosity. Live in service of one another. Love one another as I have loved you."

While His message is clear, the practice of serving others is difficult at best. It goes against every self-preserving, self-regarding instinct that we have. The world says the greatest love is to love ourselves. The world says that the pursuit of becoming an idol is a noble thing to do. But Scripture says, "Clothe yourselves, all of you, with humility toward one another, for 'God opposes the proud but gives grace to the humble.' Humble yourselves, therefore, under the mighty hand of God so that at the proper time he may exalt you" (1 Peter 5:5–6 ESV).

We are all broken, proud, and selfish. It is the human condition, and it is made manifest through incessant self-obsession. The world continually preaches to us the "me, mine, my thoughts, my feelings, my hopes, my dreams, my stuff, my, me-me-me" philosophy of self-actualization. Every song, movie, and self-help guru loudly sends the message of "just be yourself, and you will finally be happy." And while there is absolutely value in authentically accepting ourselves as an utterly unique, infinitely valuable, unconditionally loved soul made in the image of God, the message of self-obsession will only lead us to a dead end of disappointment. Because when we finally get to the place that was supposed to make us happy, we are still lost. We are still broken and small. And we still need a Savior. What defines us is not what other people think of us, nor is it what we feel about ourselves. It is what God has said about us. And it is eternally confirmed by what Christ has done for us. We are infinitely important and loved because He says we are. And that is something that emotion, circumstance, or society can never take away.

Humility is in short supply. As a matter fact, as soon we believe we are humble, we most certainly are not. We can live in pursuit of humility as long as we don't think we have arrived at humility. Jesus modeled for us the best way to push aside the suffocating self-regard that is so deeply ingrained in us all. We do this by service. We do this when we give ourselves away without expectation or compensation. There is no other way.

I say all this as a living and breathing hypocrite. It is one thing to observe what is so apparent in the life of Christ. It is quite another to follow Him into that kind of self-sacrifice. This may be the most challenging aspect of Jesus-like life for me to personally imitate. Ask my wife and my children. But it is a journey I am pursuing nonetheless. By God's grace, I will start to see those Jesus opportunities more often, and I will have the courage to push aside my agenda and desires to serve out of love rather than obligation. The truth is, we *all* have to start somewhere.

As we follow after Jesus, we will find ourselves in situations and circumstances where we can serve selflessly. His spirit within us will guide us and lead us if we will slow down and listen. Genuine freedom can be found when we are no longer defending our rights and entitlements and instead we are giving ourselves to the needs of others. This is a lifelong journey of transformation. There are no shortcuts. But there is joy to be found as we follow Jesus into the needs of the ones He loves all around us. The practices of this following week are there to be a catalyst to the more profound Jesus-like life. As always, this is a starter that we will pursue for the rest of our lives. The goal is not a false humility in the guise of self-deprecation or self-flagellation. The goal is to see our Hero, Jesus, in the eyes of others and to serve Him through serving them.

Jesus Served

MEMORIZE WEEKLY

Now that I, your Lord and Teacher, have washed your feet, you also should wash one another's feet. I have set you an example that you should do as I have done for you.
—John 13:14–15 (NIV)

Focus Daily: (Read the above verse.)

Focus Questions: In one of Jesus's last interactions with His disciples, He did the most menial task you can do for another in that culture. He washed their feet. In that same evening he instituted communion, the sharing of bread and wine to remember His sacrifice for sin. Why do you suppose He paired these images together?

Practice Daily: Remember, as always, our posture in these practices is to create space for intimacy with God and with other people. Choose someone you are close to today to serve. It could be a family member, a coworker, or a neighbor. Find some way to meet a need for them without their knowing. Then write about the experience in your journal entry.

JOURNAL DAILY

(Write at least three sentences per day):

Jesus Served

MEMORIZE WEEKLY

Now that I, your Lord and Teacher, have washed your feet, you also should wash one another's feet. I have set you an example that you should do as I have done for you.
—John 13:14–15 (NIV)

Focus Daily: "Again, the devil took Him to a very high mountain and showed him all the kingdoms of the world and their splendor. 'All this I will give you,' he said, 'if you will bow down and worship me.' Jesus said to him, 'Away from me, Satan! For it is written, "Worship the Lord your God, and serve him only"'" (Matthew 4:8–10 NIV).

Focus Questions: Satan tempted Jesus with the kingdoms of this world. He asked Jesus to use His power to serve Himself. In your personal life, how do you see this temptation surface? When is it OK to use your authority to serve yourself, and when is it a problem?

Practice Daily: Look for an opportunity today to serve a stranger. Maybe it is something as simple as letting them in your lane on the freeway. Or it might be something that costs you. Pray and ask God to reveal that opportunity for you today.

JOURNAL DAILY

(Write at least three sentences per day):

_____

_____

_____

_____

_____

_____

_____

_____

_____

_____

_____

_____

_____

_____

_____

_____

_____

_____

Jesus Served

MEMORIZE WEEKLY

Now that I, your Lord and Teacher, have washed your feet, you also should wash one another's feet. I have set you an example that you should do as I have done for you.
—John 13:14–15 (NIV)

Focus Daily: "Jesus called them together and said, 'You know that the rulers of the Gentiles lord it over them, and their high officials exercise authority over them. Not so with you. Instead, whoever wants to become great among you must be your servant, and whoever wants to be first must be your slave—just as the Son of Man did not come to be served, but to serve, and to give his life as a ransom for many'" (Matthew 20:25–28 NIV).

Focus Questions: Is it OK to seek greatness? If you serve in order to gain true greatness, is that a self-serving motive? Did Jesus serve others in order to elevate Himself?

Practice Daily: Here is where it begins to get hard. Who is that difficult person in your daily rhythm? Perhaps a coworker or a snarky person at the lunch counter? It might even be a family member. Pray and ask God to review an opportunity for you to serve them without expectation sometime today or tomorrow. See if you can do it anonymously. How can you bless that challenging person?

JOURNAL DAILY

(Write at least three sentences per day):

Jesus Served

MEMORIZE WEEKLY

Now that I, your Lord and Teacher, have washed your feet, you also should wash one another's feet. I have set you an example that you should do as I have done for you.
—John 13:14–15 (NIV)

Focus Daily: "Do nothing out of selfish ambition or vain conceit. Rather, in humility value others above yourselves, not looking to your own interests but each of you to the interests of the others. In your relationships with one another, have the same mindset as Christ Jesus" (Philippians 2:3–5 NIV).

Focus Questions: The apostle Paul encourages us to serve people the way Jesus serves people. He tells us we can have the same mindset as Christ. How hard is it to see another person's goals or interests above your own? Have you ever turned your attention from something that was important to you to listen to someone talk about something you didn't really care about? What did that feel like?

Practice Daily: If you haven't served that difficult person yet, today is the day. Make it a top priority for yourself. Then write about the experience in your journal entry, knowing you will tell someone about the experience later in the week.

JOURNAL DAILY

(Write at least three sentences per day):

_____

_____

_____

_____

_____

_____

_____

_____

_____

_____

_____

_____

_____

_____

_____

_____

_____

_____

_____

_____

Jesus Served

MEMORIZE WEEKLY

Now that I, your Lord and Teacher, have
washed your feet, you also should wash one
another's feet. I have set you an example that
you should do as I have done for you.
—John 13:14–15 (NIV)

Focus Daily: "Carry each other's burdens, and in this way you will fulfill
the law of Christ" (Galatians 6:2 NIV).

Focus Questions: What does it mean to carry the burdens of another
person? Is the author speaking metaphorically or literally? How does
this fulfill the law of Christ?

Practice Daily: Today ask a number of people how they are doing, with
the agenda of actually finding out how they are doing. Ask them more
than yes-or-no questions, and listen closely for the burden that they
carry. Lift those people's burdens up in prayer today as another way to
serve them.

JOURNAL DAILY

(Write at least three sentences per day):

Jesus Served

MEMORIZE WEEKLY

Now that I, your Lord and Teacher, have
washed your feet, you also should wash one
another's feet. I have set you an example that
you should do as I have done for you.
—John 13:14–15 (NIV)

Focus Daily: "Clothe yourselves, all of you, with humility toward one another, for 'God opposes the proud but gives grace to the humble.' Humble yourselves, therefore, under the mighty hand of God so that at the proper time he may exalt you" (1 Peter 5:5–6 ESV).

Focus Questions: How are service and humility related to one another? What does it mean for God to oppose pride?

Practice Daily: How did this practice challenge you? Did you find yourself resistant in one of the situations you faced? Did you find it a humbling experience? Who was easy to serve, and who was difficult to serve? Write down the answers to these questions in your journal with the knowledge that you will share them with someone close to you or with your study group. Ask God once again to put someone in your path today whom you can meaningfully serve.

JOURNAL DAILY
(Write at least three sentences per day):

Jesus Asked Questions

In the Gospels Jesus asks many more questions than he answers. To be precise, Jesus asks 307 questions. He is asked 183 of which he only answers 3. Asking questions was central to Jesus' life and teachings.
—Martin B. Copenhaver

"J esus is the answer for the world today" goes the old American gospel song from the '70s. And He most certainly is. When we examine the nature of Jesus's teaching, we see that He is not only the answer, but perhaps He is also the question. Jesus almost never answered a question directly in the Gospels. Instead, He used questions to provoke thought, to encourage, to challenge, and to inform. Some of those include the following:

What are you looking for?

Who are you looking for?

What do you want?

What is your name?

Why are you afraid?

Why do you worry?

If you love those who love you, what credit is that to you?

What do you want me to do for you?

Who do people say I am?

What are you talking about?

What do you think about the Christ?

Why do think evil is in your hearts?

The list goes on to include more than 300 questions that Jesus posed to people. They range from something as simple as "What are you looking for?" to "Why would people gain the whole world but lose their lives?"

Born out of rabbinic tradition, the culture of Jesus's day often used rhetorical and open ended questions as powerful devices for dialogue. But when Jesus asked questions, His purpose went beyond the device of language. His intent was to teach us all to ask better questions, not only of others but also ourselves. It is interesting to note that Jesus was rarely satisfied with a yes-or-no answer. His questions were poignant and incisive. His questions went beyond small talk at a dinner party. And His questions were considerate of the other person while at the same time unafraid to challenge his or her thinking. Jesus never shied away from asking questions that would reveal one's heart as well as one's motives.

> Why do you look at the speck of sawdust in your brother's eye and pay no attention to the plank in your own eye? How can you say to your brother, "Let me take the speck out of your eye," when all the time there is a plank in your own eye? (Matthew 7:3–4 NIV)

> How can you believe since you accept glory from one another but do not seek the glory that comes from the only God? (John 5:44 NIV)

> If you love those who love you, what reward will you get? (Matthew 5:46 NIV)

These kinds of questions are a gut check, a way of first examining our own thinking. More often than not, the things we are critical of in other people are things we find in ourselves. And Jesus challenges us to examine our motives and subconscious judgments by some simple questions. We can learn to ask better questions of ourselves before we evaluate other people.

Jesus also taught us to ask questions generously. Throughout Scripture, He asked questions of genuine interest. In the same way, when we inquire of someone else, we show how we value them and love them. We are all intensely interested in our own thinking and concerns. But Jesus taught us to turn that energy toward other people, to see beneath the external façade, and to stay long enough to ask and listen and ask again. "What is your name?" "Why are you worried?" "What are you looking for?" "What do you want me to do for you?"

These are not casual questions asked in passing. They will require time and emotional investment. As we learned in previous chapters, love doesn't happen in a hurry. We can't listen in a hurry. And we can't pose thoughtful questions in a hurry. It can take time to get real answers.

In Jesus's own authority, He asked questions as a means to teach others. But we need to be cautious with this mechanism. We can approach people with this posture when they are in a position to receive from us. It may be with our children or with those with whom we have some kind of mentoring relationship. But it would be a mistake to approach our peers in this way because it would be likely viewed as condescending and potentially self-righteous. Jesus can do this because of who He is. We are not nearly there. We ask these kinds of questions with the posture of "one beggar showing another beggar where to find bread." And we must approach people through humility and the leading of the Holy Spirit. We must ask ourselves the questios, "Does this person have ears to hear? What is the most loving question I can ask? Have I earned the right to speak into this person's life?"

> When he had finished washing their feet, he put on his clothes and returned to his place. "Do you understand what I have done for you?" he asked them. (John 13:12 NIV)

> Whoever lives by believing in me will never die. Do you believe this? (John 11:26 NIV)

> Why do you call me "Lord, Lord," and do not do what I say? (Luke 6:46 NIV)

Can the blind lead the blind? Will they not both fall into a pit? (Luke 6:39 NIV)

Which of these three do you think was a neighbor to the man who fell into the hands of robbers? (Luke 10:36 NIV)

What can anyone give in exchange for their soul? (Mark 8:37 NIV)

Do you believe in the Son of Man? (John 9:35 NIV)

Jesus asked no trivial questions. And we would all do well to open our hearts and answer these questions for ourselves. Jesus is always piercing through our layers of identity to reveal our true selves, the true selves that must find healing in Him. Most lovingly, the Savior uses questions to peel away all of the false layers like an onion. And as He does this, as uncomfortable as it may be, He sets us free to be who He is calling us to be and not who the world says we are.

As we follow our Hero, we will learn to ask better questions. We will ask better questions of ourselves. And we will ask better questions of others. Such is the path we walk when we follow closely behind the Savior.

Jesus Asked Questions

MEMORIZE WEEKLY

Jesus said to her, "I am the resurrection and the life. The one who believes in me will live, even though they die; and whoever lives by believing in me will never die. Do you believe this?"
—John 11:25–26 (NIV)

Focus Daily: (Read the above verse.)

Focus Questions: To know Him is to love Him. To love Him is to trust Him. Jesus makes an enormous statement about Himself. What do you think "the resurrection and the life" means? Do you believe it? When do you doubt?

Practice Daily: Remember, as always, our posture in these practices is to create space for intimacy with God and with other people. Love is always the context. Go through the list of questions Jesus asks listed on the first page of this chapter and write down the answers in your journal entry today.

JOURNAL DAILY

(Write at least three sentences per day):

_____

_____

_____

_____

_____

_____

_____

_____

_____

_____

_____

_____

_____

_____

_____

_____

_____

_____

_____

Jesus Asked Questions

MEMORIZE WEEKLY

Jesus said to her, "I am the resurrection and the life. The one who believes in me will live, even though they die; and whoever lives by believing in me will never die. Do you believe this?"
—John 11:25–26 (NIV)

Focus Daily: "Why do you call me "Lord, Lord,' and do not do what I say?" (Luke 6:46 NIV).

Focus Questions: What area of your life does this question address? Why do you suppose it is a challenge for you?

Practice Daily: Read Luke 6:46–49. Journal about a couple of moments when your "house fell." What was the situation that you held back from God? How would it have been different had you submitted to Him?

JOURNAL DAILY

(Write at least three sentences per day):

_____

_____

_____

_____

_____

_____

_____

_____

_____

_____

_____

_____

_____

_____

_____

_____

_____

_____

Jesus Asked Questions

MEMORIZE WEEKLY
Jesus said to her, "I am the resurrection and the life. The one who believes in me will live, even though they die; and whoever lives by believing in me will never die. Do you believe this?"
—John 11:25–26 (NIV)

Focus Daily: "Why do you look at the speck of sawdust in your brother's eye and pay no attention to the plank in your own eye? How can you say to your brother, 'Let me take the speck out of your eye,' when all the time there is a plank in your own eye? You hypocrite, first take the plank out of your own eye, and then you will see clearly to remove the speck from your brother's eye" (Matthew 7:3–5 NIV).

Focus Questions: Jesus asks us to focus our faultfinding on ourselves before someone else. Have you ever caught yourself critical of someone for something you do? How did that affect the way you see that other person?

Practice Daily: In Mark 9 Jesus asks, "What is your name?" In the ancient world names were pregnant with meaning and immensely important to an individual's sense of identity. Make a point today of learning the names of three people whom you see frequently but whose names you've never learned.

JOURNAL DAILY

(Write at least three sentences per day):

_____

_____

_____

_____

_____

_____

_____

_____

_____

_____

_____

_____

_____

_____

_____

_____

_____

_____

Jesus Asked Questions

MEMORIZE WEEKLY

Jesus said to her, "I am the resurrection and the life. The one who believes in me will live, even though they die; and whoever lives by believing in me will never die. Do you believe this?"
—John 11:25–26 (NIV)

Focus Daily: "Why do you worry . . . ?" (Matthew 6:28 NIV).

Focus Questions: What is it that you worry about? What takes up your emotional energy? How long has this been a concern for you?

Practice Daily: Today read Matthew 6:25–34 and make a point to inquire of someone how they are actually doing. Don't be satisfied with the answer of "fine" or "OK." Ask them if they have any worries for which you could pray. Write down those worries and make a point of praying for them before the end of the day. If it seems appropriate, pray for them out loud in front of that person.

JOURNAL DAILY

(Write at least three sentences per day):

Jesus Asked Questions

MEMORIZE WEEKLY

Jesus said to her, "I am the resurrection and the life. The one who believes in me will live, even though they die; and whoever lives by believing in me will never die. Do you believe this?"
—John 11:25–26 (NIV)

Focus Daily: "What do you think about the Messiah . . . ?" (Matthew 22:42 NIV).

Focus Questions: How would you articulate who Jesus is to someone who has never heard of Him? How would you explain your relationship with Jesus to someone who used to go to church?

Practice Daily: Look for an opportunity to talk about Jesus today. Ask someone what his or her opinion is in regard to Jesus. Do this without a response or defense. Ask the question with the only agenda of caring about what he or she has to say and a desire to understand.

JOURNAL DAILY

(Write at least three sentences per day):

Jesus Asked Questions

MEMORIZE WEEKLY

Jesus said to her, "I am the resurrection and the life. The one who believes in me will live, even though they die; and whoever lives by believing in me will never die. Do you believe this?"
—John 11:25–26 (NIV)

Focus Daily: "Jesus, knowing all that was going to happen to him, went out and asked them, 'Who is it you want?'" (John 18:4 NIV).

Focus Questions: Who do you want? Who do you want to be associated with? What group of people do you wish included you?

Practice Daily: As you interact with someone today, look for an opportunity for deeper conversation. Ask this person these questions: What kind of person do you want to be? What do you want out of life? Is there a person you wish you were closer to?

JOURNAL DAILY

(Write at least three sentences per day):

_____

_____

_____

_____

_____

_____

_____

_____

_____

_____

_____

_____

_____

_____

_____

_____

_____

_____

Jesus Loved People

God loves each of us as if there were only one of us.
—Augustine

Love is the context for everything good. It is the foundation. It is the engine. It is the rocket fuel. It is the water in which the good fish swims. It is the sun that makes the good grass green. God is love.

Jesus made it clear that love was central to His life and teaching. He doesn't have a finite amount of it. It is not a zero-sum game. It doesn't run out. It doesn't falter. It doesn't show favoritism. It doesn't keep a ledger of wrongdoing. It doesn't give up. It is overflowing, unconditional, and extravagant.

> [The Pharisees asked,] "'Teacher, which is the greatest commandment in the Law?'
>
> And Jesus replied: "'Love the Lord your God with all your heart and with all your soul and with all your mind.' This is the first and greatest commandment. And the second is like it: 'Love your neighbor as yourself.' All the Law and the Prophets hang on these two commandments.'" (Matthew 22:36–40 NIV)

We talked about this in the opening chapter of our journey together. Seeing all of the practices as a way of exercising love for God and love for people will be the healthiest and most sustainable approach we can have. It is easy to say and difficult to do. We can't remind ourselves enough of how much He loves and accepts us and how much He expects us to love and accept other people. We tend to drift toward earning God's love and expecting other people to earn our love. The drift is real and happens to everyone. And while God's grace and love can seem so immense that it appears too good to be true, it is not. If anyone wants to see what love looks like, one only need look at the life of Jesus. He shows us observably what it is to love God and to love others the way you love yourself.

In the above Scripture, the Pharisees asked Jesus which commandment was greatest. He answered that to love God was the greatest commandment. But before they could pat Him on the back for answering rightly, He added to it. He coupled the love of other people with the love of God correctly. The two cannot be separated. It is far too easy to say we love God privately while having a public disdain for His kids, and while the love of God can be abstract, the love of other people is concrete. Jesus spelled it out as He set the precedent that the love of God would ultimately be expressed in the love of His kids: "My command is this: Love each other as I have loved you" (John 15:12 NIV).

Jesus made it crystal clear that this new covenant was completely dependent on love, replacing the old ways and making them obsolete. Love would be the law of His Kingdom, and everything else would be commentary. The rest of the New Testament Scriptures are an extrapolation of this covenant. In other words, they provide examples of how it is worked out while being grounded, interpreted, and filtered through the love of Jesus.

The apostle John said it this way: "We love because he first loved us. Whoever claims to love God yet hates a brother or sister is a liar. For whoever does not love their brother and sister, whom they have seen, cannot love God, whom they have not seen. And he has given us this command: Anyone who loves God must also love their brother and sister" (1 John 4:19–21 NIV).

The way we are to love God is to love other people as Jesus loves us. We are kidding ourselves if we think it works any other way. But if we are to love "our neighbors as we love ourselves," who is our neighbor?

Jesus was asked this question by experts in the law, and as usual, he answered it by telling a story and gave us the parable of the good Samaritan. To summarize, a man was robbed and left bleeding on the side of the road. He was passed by two religious people who didn't have the time or desire to help him out. Then he was helped by a Samaritan, somebody he didn't like and whom he found offensive. Then Jesus asked, "Who was a neighbor to this man?" They answered, "It was the man who helped." And Jesus replied, "Go and do likewise."

In Matthew 5:46–47, Jesus said, "If you love only those who love you, what reward is there for that? Even corrupt tax collectors do that much. If you are kind only to your friends, how are you different from anyone else? Even pagans do that" (NLT).

We like people who like us. And we like people who are like us. Everybody does. We don't have to follow Jesus to be nice to our friends. But the love of Christ compels us to love those who are different from us. It drives us to open our hearts to people we dislike and with whom we disagree. We may be offended by their lifestyle, their morals, their politics, their appearance, or their attitudes toward us, but that does not take away our responsibility to respond to them in love. Jesus elaborated a bit more in the Gospel of Luke.

> If you love those who love you, what credit is that to you? Even sinners love those who love them. And if you do good to those who are good to you, what credit is that to you? Even sinners do that. And if you lend to those from whom you expect repayment, what credit is that to you? Even sinners lend to sinners, expecting to be repaid in full. But love your enemies, do good to them, and lend to them without expecting to get anything back. Then your reward will be great, and you will be children of the Most High, because he is kind to the ungrateful and wicked. Be merciful, just as your Father is merciful." (Luke 6:32–36 NIV)

That's a pretty high bar. It's one thing to love people who are in our path. It's quite another to love people who are blocking our path. They're the same kind of people who shouted insults and jeered at Jesus while He was dying on the cross. His response was, "Father, forgive them. They don't know what they're doing."

A good friend of mine received some counsel from his grandma. She said, "You don"t have to like everybody. But you gotta love everybody." These are wise words from Grandma. That is the kind of wisdom that comes from a lifetime of following Jesus and observing the nature of humanity. It is that kind of Jesus-love that defuses animosity and builds bridges where there is division. It is that kind of love that drove the early Christ followers to serve their Roman oppressors who were dying of plague and rescue Roman children who had been disposed of in the dumps. And it is that Jesus-love that compels us to reach across the political, cultural, and religious divides to love those who are unlike us and whom we may not like: "For Christ's love compels us, because we are convinced that one died for all, and therefore all died. And he died for all, that those who live should no longer live for themselves but for him who died for them and was raised again" (2 Corinthians 5:14–15 NIV).

The love of Jesus is self-sacrificial and generous. As we follow our Hero, we will learn to love as He did. It won't come overnight; it is a life-long journey. We will likely start with the people under our own roof. As we grow in intimacy with Him, He transforms and empowers us to love outside of our comfort zones in word and action. As we grow in Him, His love will mark us like a tattoo. It will be the one distinguishing characteristic that identifies us with our Hero.

> "A new command I give you: Love one another. As I have loved you, so you must love one another. By this everyone will know that you are my disciples, if you love one another."

(John 13:34-35 NIV)

Jesus could pick anything to be the big identifier of his followers. He could've picked biblical education, sin management, church attendance. He could've picked character traits like kindness or just plain being a "good person" relative to everyone else.

Instead, He said, "Love people the way I have loved you. Love people even when they don't respond in turn. Love them when they are nice to you. And, love them when they are not. Love without expectation. This will fulfill all the requirements of holiness. And it is this kind of love that will point people beyond you to me. You just go ahead and love people, and I will be responsible for the consequences."

Jesus Loved People

MEMORIZE WEEKLY

Jesus replied: "'Love the Lord your God with all your heart and with all your soul and with all your mind.' This is the first and greatest commandment. And the second is like it: 'Love your neighbor as yourself.' All the Law and the Prophets hang on these two commandments."
—Matthew 22:37–40 (NIV)

Focus Daily: (Read the above verse.)

Focus Questions: Does this simplify things for you? Or is it more intimidating? Is it easier to follow a set of rules or to try to love people the way you love yourself?

Practice Daily: Remember, as always, our posture in these practices is to create space for intimacy with God and with other people. Love is always the context. Read 1 Corinthians 13:4–7, then pray through the same verses through the lens of how God loves you—for example, "God is patient with me. God is kind to me." Afterward, choose a family member or friend and pray that you can love him or her that same way. Walk through each verse with that person in mind.

JOURNAL DAILY

(Write at least three sentences per day):

_____

_____

_____

_____

_____

_____

_____

_____

_____

_____

_____

_____

_____

_____

_____

_____

Jesus Loved People

MEMORIZE WEEKLY

Jesus replied: "'Love the Lord your God with all your heart and with all your soul and with all your mind.' This is the first and greatest commandment. And the second is like it: 'Love your neighbor as yourself.' All the Law and the Prophets hang on these two commandments."
—Matthew 22:37–40 (NIV)

Focus Daily: "Dear friends, let us love one another, for love comes from God. Everyone who loves has been born of God and knows God. Whoever does not love does not know God, because God is love. This is how God showed his love among us: He sent his one and only Son into the world that we might live through him. This is love: not that we loved God, but that he loved us and sent his Son as an atoning sacrifice for our sins. Dear friends, since God so loved us, we also ought to love one another. No one has ever seen God; but if we love one another, God lives in us and his love is made complete in us" (1 John 4:7–12 NIV).

Focus Questions: Have you seen evidence of the absence of love in the absence of God? What does that look like? How is God's love made complete in us when we love one another?

Practice Daily: Pray through this portion of Scripture, and ask God to reveal where you are loving and where you were not loving in your circle of influence. Write down below how He is calling you to follow Him in this regard.

JOURNAL DAILY
(Write at least three sentences per day):

_____

_____

_____

_____

_____

_____

_____

_____

_____

_____

_____

_____

_____

_____

Jesus Loved People

MEMORIZE WEEKLY

Jesus replied: "'Love the Lord your God with all your heart and with all your soul and with all your mind.' This is the first and greatest commandment. And the second is like it: 'Love your neighbor as yourself.' All the Law and the Prophets hang on these two commandments."
—Matthew 22:37–40 (NIV)

Focus Daily: "We love because he first loved us. Whoever claims to love God yet hates a brother or sister is a liar. For whoever does not love their brother and sister, whom they have seen, cannot love God, whom they have not seen. And he has given us this command: Anyone who loves God must also love their brother and sister" (1 John 4:19–2 NIV).

Focus Questions: Is it harder or easier to love the people to whom we are closest? Why? What is John saying about love for God and love for people?

Practice Daily: Pray through this portion of Scripture, and ask God to reveal to you the names of people whom you have a difficult time liking. What would it look like for you to love them well? Journal those observations below.

JOURNAL DAILY

(Write at least three sentences per day):

Jesus Loved People

MEMORIZE WEEKLY

Jesus replied: "'Love the Lord your God with
all your heart and with all your soul and with
all your mind.' This is the first and greatest
commandment. And the second is like it: 'Love
your neighbor as yourself.' All the Law and the
Prophets hang on these two commandments."
—Matthew 22:37–40 (NIV)

Focus Daily: "As the Father has loved me, so have I loved you. Now remain in my love. If you keep my commands, you will remain in my love, just as I have kept my Father's commands and remain in his love. I have told you this so that my joy may be in you and that your joy may be complete. My command is this: Love each other as I have loved you. Greater love has no one than this: to lay down one's life for one's friends" (John 15:9–13 NIV).

Focus Questions: What does it look like to "remain" in God's love? What did Jesus mean when He said, "your joy may be complete"?

Practice Daily: Look at the names you journaled about yesterday. You wrote down an idea of what it would look like to love them well. This is something in word and in deed. Write the name of one person from that list here: _____. Make a plan to express love for them by the end of the week. It may be something as simple as forgiving them for a hurt, or it may require some self-sacrificial action on your part. Write your plan below.

JOURNAL DAILY
(Write at least three sentences per day):

_____

_____

_____

_____

_____

_____

_____

_____

_____

_____

_____

_____

_____

_____

_____

Jesus Loved People

MEMORIZE WEEKLY

Jesus replied: "'Love the Lord your God with all your heart and with all your soul and with all your mind.' This is the first and greatest commandment. And the second is like it: 'Love your neighbor as yourself.' All the Law and the Prophets hang on these two commandments."
—Matthew 22:37–40 (NIV)

Focus Daily: "You have heard that it was said, 'Love your neighbor and hate your enemy.' But I tell you, love your enemies and pray for those who persecute you, that you may be children of your Father in heaven. He causes his sun to rise on the evil and the good, and sends rain on the righteous and the unrighteous. If you love those who love you, what reward will you get? Are not even the tax collectors doing that? And if you greet only your own people, what are you doing more than others? Do not even pagans do that?" (Matthew 5:43–47 NIV)

Focus Questions: This is a hard teaching from Jesus. Is He saying we should love people with some kind of reward in mind? How does praying for your enemy make you a child of "your Father in heaven?"

Practice Daily: Today take a concrete step toward executing your plan from yesterday. Ask a friend to pray for you and hold you accountable.

JOURNAL DAILY

(Write at least three sentences per day):

_____

_____

_____

_____

_____

_____

_____

_____

_____

_____

_____

_____

_____

_____

_____

_____

_____

_____

Jesus Loved People

MEMORIZE WEEKLY

Jesus replied: "'Love the Lord your God with all your heart and with all your soul and with all your mind.' This is the first and greatest commandment. And the second is like it: 'Love your neighbor as yourself.' All the Law and the Prophets hang on these two commandments."
—Matthew 22:37–40 (NIV)

Focus Daily: "This is how we know what love is: Jesus Christ laid down his life for us. And we ought to lay down our lives for our brothers and sisters. If anyone has material possessions and sees a brother or sister in need but has no pity on them, how can the love of God be in that person? Dear children, let us not love with words or speech but with actions and in truth" (1 John 3:16–18 NIV).

Focus Questions: Is God saying to love other people is to love Himself? Why or why not? Can love for God and love for others be separated based on this week's experience? Is love an emotion, or is it action?

Practice Daily: What did you do to love your challenging person? How did that feel? How did that affect the way you see Christ's love? Write your answer below.

JOURNAL DAILY

(Write at least three sentences per day):

_____

_____

_____

_____

_____

_____

_____

_____

_____

_____

_____

_____

_____

_____

_____

_____

_____

_____

Jesus Entered In

The incarnation is a kind of vast joke whereby the
Creator of the ends of the earth comes among us in
diapers. . . . Until we too have taken the idea of the
God-man seriously enough to be scandalized by it,
we have not taken it as seriously as it demands to be
taken.
—Frederick Buechner

I n Jesus, God came close. And in doing so, He entered into the messi-
ness of our lives in the most profound way. He didn't keep us at a distance. Instead, He breathed and bled. He toiled and tired. He came
so close that our mess covered Him.

I once heard a leader say that we are to isolate ourselves completely
from non-Christians because Scripture says, "Come out from among
them and be ye separate" (2 Corinthians 6:17 KJV). If we believe that
Jesus is the fulfillment of all Scripture and the example of perfect holiness, what does that mean? What does it look like if we are to "come
out from among them and be ye separate"? As always, Jesus is the lens
through which we see all of Scripture, both Old and New Testaments.
Jesus demonstrated what it looks like to fulfill all holiness in the context
of the perfect love of God.

"For our sake he made him to be sin
who knew no sin, so that in him we
might become the righteousness
of God."

(2 Corinthians 5:21 ESV)

Jesus showed us the measure of real holiness and what relationship that holiness has with a world that so desperately needs Him. The holiness of Jesus isn't afraid of the mess. It isn't afraid to get dirty. It isn't afraid to appear guilty by association. It isn't afraid to touch the untouchable. Instead, His holiness enters in and elevates everyone it touches.

What my well-intentioned friend missed in quoting the apostle Paul was that both Paul and Isaiah were referring to idol worship. That to "come out from among them" means we don't worship the things that they worship. So Jesus came close to the people who needed a Savior and pointed them away from worshiping false things. He drew them to himself to bring them the life that their idols could never deliver.

While on earth, Jesus called all kinds of people to Himself, and the religious leaders of His day resented him for it. Famously, Jesus invited a tax collector to be among his chosen twelve disciples, and the people were astonished that He would associate Himself in any way with that kind of person.

After this, Jesus went out and saw a tax collector by the name of Levi sitting at his tax booth. "Follow me," Jesus said to him, and Levi got up, left everything and followed him.

Then Levi held a great banquet for Jesus at his house, and a large crowd of tax collectors and others were eating with them. But the Pharisees and the teachers of the law who belonged to their sect complained to his disciples, "Why do you eat and drink with tax collectors and sinners?"

Jesus answered them, "It is not the healthy who need a doctor, but the sick. I have not come to call the righteous, but sinners to repentance." (Luke 5:27–31 NIV)

And again, from Matthew 11:19: "The Son of Man came eating and drinking, and they say, 'Here is a glutton and a drunkard, a friend of tax collectors and sinners!' But wisdom is provden by her deeds" (NIV).

Just as He entered into the lives of the tax collector, the leper, and the prostitute, Jesus entered into humanity in every way. He celebrated with others. He grieved with others. He spent time at parties. He spent time with the dying. And He got so close to sinners that he was accused of being just like them. But Jesus was not afraid of the accusation. His love overwhelmed any concern for Himself or the perceptions of the self-righteous.

In the same way, we see Him celebrating joyously with all kinds of people, including those who would be considered unacceptable outsiders in His culture. But Jesus loved them equally. Instead of being dragged down by their brokenness, His love brought them up out of sin and depravity. Jesus's love accepts everyone where they are without leaving them where they are.

As much as Jesus celebrated with others, He also grieved with others. He hurts as we hurt. He weeps when we weep. And He roars in anger at death itself, as demonstrated when His friend Lazarus died. Isaiah 53:3 even says that He was "a man of suffering, and familiar with pain. Like one from whom people hide their faces he was despised, and we held him in low esteem" (NIV). By the thousands, He touched those who were deemed untouchable. He spent nearly all of His time with the poor, the sick, and the destitute. He even equated service to the outsider with serving Himself. In the parable of the sheep and the goats, He demonstrated how:

"For I was hungry and you gave me something to eat, I was thirsty and you gave me something to drink, I was a stranger and you invited me in, I needed clothes and you clothed me, I was sick and you looked after me, I was in prison and you came to visit me.

Then the righteous will answer him, "Lord, when did we see you hungry and feed you, or thirsty and give you something to drink? When did we see you a stranger and invite you in, or needing clothes and clothe you? When did we see you sick or in prison and go to visit you?"

The King will reply, "Truly I tell you, whatever you did for one of the least of these brothers and sisters of mine, you did for me." (Matthew 25:35–40 NIV)

The love of Jesus came close. And as we follow Him, He will lead us places we never expected to go and spend time with people we never planned to meet. This is the challenge and adventure of following our Hero. He calls us to enter into the mess and joy of the lives all around us.

The apostle Paul elucidated this in the book of Romans. As we read this through the lens of Jesus's love, the text comes alive:

Do not conform to the pattern of this world, but be transformed by the renewing of your mind. Then you will be able to test and approve what God's will is—his good, pleasing and perfect will.

For by the grace given me I say to every one of you: Do not think of yourself more highly than you ought, but rather think of yourself with sober judgment, in accordance with the faith God has distributed to each of you. . . .

Love must be sincere. Hate what is evil; cling to what is good. . . .

Bless those who persecute you; bless and do not curse. *Rejoice with those who rejoice; mourn with those who mourn.* Live in harmony with one another. Do not be proud, but be willing to associate with people of low position. Do not be conceited. . . .

Do not be overcome by evil, but overcome evil with good." Romans 12:2–3, 9, 14–16, 21 NIV, emphasis aded)

The world will always beg us to look out for ourselves. It will encourage us to seek the company of people who will make us look good, who will advance our career paths, and who will elevate our reputations. But to have our minds renewed and transformed by the love of Jesus will cause us to see every soul in our paths as one that is loved and made in the image of God. We realize that as we enter into those lives, compelled by the love of Christ, we do indeed "rejoice with those who rejoice and mourn with those who mourn" just as our Hero did.

And yet we do need to be cautious of loving the things of the world more than the things of God. The apostle John warned us in his letter that loving the things, the values, the ethics, the offerings of the world that are rooted in self-service of every kind will corrupt us. They will dilute and divide our hearts from what is most important as we follow Jesus. It is possible to enter into people's lives to love them and serve them without agreeing with them. We can be in relationship with someone without condoning their values or behavior. We can affirm them as a human being. And we can love and support them while following Jesus. Because His holiness in us will love others exactly where they are. And it is that love that will draw them beyond us to Himself.

Jesus Entered In

MEMORIZE WEEKLY

Rejoice with those who rejoice; mourn
with those who mourn.
—Romans 12:15 (NIV)

Focus Daily: (Read the above verse.)

Focus Questions: Is it difficult to celebrate someone else's successes?
When someone else is having a great season, do you find yourself
comparing your life to theirs?

Practice Daily: Remember, as always, our posture in these practices is to
create space for intimacy with God and with other people. Love is always
the context. This week we will consciously try to enter into the joys and
difficulties of the people around us. In today's journal entry, write down
the names of one or two people with whom you can celebrate and one
or two people with whom you can grieve.

JOURNAL DAILY

(Write at least three sentences per day):

Jesus Entered In

MEMORIZE WEEKLY

Rejoice with those who rejoice; mourn
with those who mourn.
—Romans 12:15 (NIV)

Focus Daily: "Live in harmony with one another. Do not be proud, but be willing to associate with people of low position. Do not be conceited" (Romans 12:16 NIV).

Focus Questions: Do you tend to gravitate to the popular or influential people in your circle? Why do you think that is? What would it look like if you sought out the person who looks most out of place in your group? How would that make you feel?

Practice Daily: Who is the person with whom you can celebrate this week? Write down how you are going to do that with him or her. It could be a note that you write or a message that you send. It could just be a few words of affirmation at the water cooler. How are you going to rejoice in this person's joy?

JOURNAL DAILY

(Write at least three sentences per day):

Jesus Entered In

MEMORIZE WEEKLY

Rejoice with those who rejoice; mourn
with those who mourn.
—Romans 12:15 (NIV)

Focus Daily: "Jesus entered Jericho and was passing through. A man was there by the name of Zacchaeus; he was a chief tax collector and was wealthy. He wanted to see who Jesus was, but because he was short he could not see over the crowd. So he ran ahead and climbed a sycamore-fig tree to see Him, since Jesus was coming that way.

When Jesus reached the spot, he looked up and said to him, 'Zacchaeus, come down immediately. I must stay at your house today.' So, he came down at once and welcomed him gladly.

All the people saw this and began to mutter, 'He has gone to be the guest of a sinner'" (Luke 19:1–7 NIV).

Focus Questions: Zacchaeus was looked down on both figuratively and literally. He was disliked by his own people for his vocation and his appearance. Who is that person in your circle of influence who is disliked for those kinds of reasons? How have you seen that person?

Practice Daily: It can be very uncomfortable to step into the pain of another person. We all tend to avoid pain whenever possible. Who is the person you identified on the first day with whom you will enter into his or her sorrow? Write down how you will do that in today's journal entry.

JOURNAL DAILY

(Write at least three sentences per day):

Jesus Entered In

MEMORIZE WEEKLY

Rejoice with those who rejoice; mourn
with those who mourn.
—**Romans 12:15 (NIV)**

Focus Daily: "Then Jesus said to his host, 'When you give a luncheon or dinner, do not invite your friends, your brothers or sisters, your relatives, or your rich neighbors; if you do, they may invite you back and so you will be repaid. But when you give a banquet, invite the poor, the crippled, the lame, the blind, and you will be blessed'" (Luke 14:12–14 NIV).

Focus Questions: When are you in a position to invite people in? How often do you have that opportunity? Have you ever invited someone to dinner or a party because you thought he or she needed a friend?

Practice Daily: Today pursue your plan to celebrate someone else's success, and write about the experience in today's journal entry.

JOURNAL DAILY

(Write at least three sentences per day):

Jesus Entered In

MEMORIZE WEEKLY

*Rejoice with those who rejoice; mourn
with those who mourn.*
—**Romans 12:15 (NIV)**

Focus Daily: "When Mary reached the place where Jesus was and saw him, she fell at his feet and said, 'Lord, if you had been here, my brother would not have died.'

When Jesus saw her weeping, and the Jews who had come along with her also weeping, he was deeply moved in spirit and troubled. 'Where have you laid him?' he asked.

'Come and see, Lord,' they replied.

Jesus wept." (John 11:32–35 NIV).

Focus Questions: Jesus already knew that He was going to raise up Lazarus and the story would have a happy ending. Knowing that, why do you think He wept?

Practice Daily: Today, pursue your plan to grieve with that person you identified already. Write about the experience in today's journal entry.

JOURNAL DAILY

(Write at least three sentences per day):

Jesus Entered In

MEMORIZE WEEKLY

Rejoice with those who rejoice; mourn
with those who mourn.
—Romans 12:15 (NIV)

Focus Daily: "Then the righteous will answer him, 'Lord, when did we see you hungry and feed you, or thirsty and give you something to drink? When did we see you a stranger and invite you in, or needing clothes and clothe you? When did we see you sick or in prison and go to visit you?'

The King will reply, 'Truly I tell you, whatever you did for one of the least of these brothers and sisters of mine, you did for me'" (Matthew 25:37–40 NIV).

Focus Questions: Why do you think Jesus equated relationship and service of outsiders with Himself? Do you find it easy or difficult to see needy people through the eyes of Christ?

Practice Daily: What opportunities do you have in your world to come close to the outsiders? Do you have access to a prison ministry or food bank? Do you know of any other opportunities to step outside your comfort zone and enter into someone else's world? Pray and ask God to reveal the path for you. Then make a plan and put it on your calendar.

JOURNAL DAILY

(Write at least three sentences per day):

_____

_____

_____

_____

_____

_____

_____

_____

_____

_____

_____

_____

_____

_____

_____

_____

_____

_____

Jesus Mentored

Tell me and I forget, teach me and I may remember,
involve me and I learn.
—Benjamin Franklin

Jesus drew crowds by the thousands. He had disciples by the hundreds. He had a dozen apostles. A small group of three. And He had one with whom He was the closest.

The life we have in Christ was never meant to be kept to ourselves. Our Hero models for us what it is to give the blessing away and to invest in others with intentionality and purpose. Jesus draws us to Himself and asks us to imitate Him. He then asks us to show others how to imitate Him.

Jesus called twelve men closest to Him and spent every waking hour with them for three years. Even among those twelve, three got more focused attention from Him. He showed them how the "with God" Kingdom life looked. He taught them in words as well as in action. They followed Him everywhere He went. And it is from these men that we have Jesus's story two thousand years later. It was through these men that Jesus birthed the movement that would outlast the Roman Empire, permeate every corner of the earth, and transform the hearts of people and the shape of nations. From a small, insignificant corner of an occupied people of an ancient empire came the most influential movement in the history of humanity. And it all started with an unknown Jewish rabbi investing in the lives of a ragtag group of unknowns.

Jesus said His kingdom would be like leaven and bread. Leaven is a very small thing that grows to the point where the entire loaf of bread is permeated and expanded. He said the Kingdom would be like a tiny seed that will grow and become so large that animals would make their homes in its branches. This is precisely what we have seen in Christianity. Jesus started with the insignificant and powerless. He poured into the lives of people and asked them to do the same to people who would, in turn, do the same. For century upon century, the world has been seeded with the gospel and the knowledge of this obscure rabbi from two thousand years ago. And we are still talking about Him in the twenty-first century because people like Peter, Andrew, James, John, Thomas, Bartholomew, and the rest passed on what they had seen and heard and asked the next generation to do the same. It is a profoundly simple and powerful plan, and Jesus invites us to participate in it.

> "Jesus came and said to them, 'All authority in heaven and on earth has been given to me. Therefore go and make disciples of all nations.'"

(Matthew 28:18–19 NIV)

Making disciples can sound extremely intimidating at first. But it is something that you grow into over a lifetime. We start in the simplest of ways and ask God to guide us. We pray that He will guide us to that person or persons in whom we will invest our lives. And we pray for Him to show us how to do it. We follow our Hero into the practice of passing along the blessing that we have been given. As Jesus has changed our lives in every conceivable way, we are compelled by love for God and love for others to do as He did.

Much has been written about this over the centuries. Scholars and leaders have dissected Jesus's method of mentoring in a hundred ways. As we grow in this practice, we will start in the most simple way we observe mentorship in the life of our Hero. There are three fundamental components.

In relationship. On common ground. By example.

Jesus didn't mentor from a distance. It was life on life. It was experience in the daily rhythm of relationship. He knew their names, their occupations, and their backgrounds. It was birthed out of friendship and love. That is the best place for any of us to start.

Who are the people in our lives that God is calling us to pour into? We don't have to pick a stranger out of a hat. They are likely right in front of us. We start by merely loving and praying for that person. It doesn't have to begin with an invitation to a Bible study or a formal discipleship program, though it may lead to something like that. It starts with the intention of giving to them what Jesus has given to us. Spend time with them and get to know their story. How did they grow up? What is their family like now? What is their relationship like with God? Then we can offer our own stories and experience with Jesus.

That said, remember that love takes time. These things don't happen quickly. It takes relational collateral for someone to allow you to speak into their spiritual life. Most of us likely know the saying, "People don't care how much you know until they know how much you care." Jesus met people in their story and their need. He accepted them and loved them before he addressed their lifestyle and behavior.

Jesus also met people on common ground. To fishermen, He spoke the fishermen's language. He went to the house of the tax collector for dinner. He spent time with a woman doing her chores at the local well. Over and over again, Jesus met people in the daily rhythm of their ordinary lives.

For you and me, it doesn't have to be a formal setting with your faith story, bullet-pointed on an index card. It starts in the coming and going of life. It can begin with common interests. We have places that we go and things that we already do that are shared by others. Maybe it's a hobby or a club. Maybe it's a sport or sports team. Whether it is in the workplace, the local coffee house, or the gym, we all have a shared space and experience with others. The common ground may even just be found in our neighborhoods or schools.

The language of a shared interest is extremely powerful. It gives us a starting place in relationship. It is the fire we gather around that opens us up to the better conversation. When we share a common experience, we have the beginning of intimacy that can grow beyond the hobby to something far more significant. At the same time, it is the love of Jesus seen in us as we share these experiences that will open the door for the better conversation. It is not a manipulation or a tactic. It is the love of Jesus poured out into the whole of our lives that bridges the gap and opens the doors. His love expressed on common ground is the foundation and beginning of a God-honoring mentor relationship.

Jesus mentored by example. It was life on life and experiential. He said, "Come follow me and watch what I do and listen to what I say. Then do the same." So they followed Him. It is likely they followed Him without necessarily believing in Him or what He had to say. They just followed. And in that following, they came to trust Him and ultimately imitate Him. They lived a lot of life together before He cut them loose to share their message with the world. He shared His life with them and then told them to go and share their lives with others. He spent enough time with them that the students eventually became the teachers.

The apostle Paul said it like this: "Follow my example, as I follow the example of Christ" (1 Corinthians 11:1 NIV).

And that is our best posture today. As we grow in our relationship with Jesus, our lives will reflect His life with growing integrity. When we become more like Him, other people will want to be more like Him. And as our intimacy with Christ transforms us, people will be drawn to what we have. There is nothing more attractive than someone who reflects the heart of Jesus. Nothing is more compelling or more convincing.

In the Sermon on the Mount, Jesus said it like this: "You are the light of the world. A city set on a hill cannot be hidden. Nor do people light a lamp and put it under a basket, but on a stand, and it gives light to all in the house. In the same way, let your light shine before others, so that they may see your good works and give glory to your Father who is in heaven" (Matthew 5:14–16 ESV).

And from the Gospel of John: "By this my Father is glorified, that you bear much fruit and so prove to be my disciples" (John 15:8 ESV).

It is the integrity of a life surrendered to Jesus and empowered by the Holy Spirit lived out loud that brings the greatest testimony and credibility to the message. By walking in intimacy and dependence on Him, He is able to bear His fruit through us. And this is the blessing we bring as His followers.

He once said, "Follow me, and I will make you fishers of men" (Matthew 4:19 ESV).

That is a promise. He's telling us that as we follow Him, we will be transformed by His love. And it is that love that will pour out of us into the lives of other people. We can't be introduced to the transformational, unconditional, extravagant love of God and keep it to ourselves. It won't be contained. It will spill out to everyone who comes in contact with us. This happens in big ways and small ways. It happens with intentionality. And it sometimes happens by accident.

But it is always centered on Jesus, born in relationship, grounded in Scripture, experienced together, and then given away to the next person. That is Jesus's plan, and He invites us into it. We get the privilege of participating in His great story by following His example. It is an adventure. And if at any time we find our spiritual lives to be boring, there is a good chance we need to take a next step deeper into our journey with Jesus. There is no greater privilege and no greater challenge. Ultimately, it is His Spirit alive in us that compels us, equips us, and moves us into the Kingdom life He would have for us all.

Jesus Mentored

MEMORIZE WEEKLY

Follow my example, as I follow the example of Christ.
—1 Corinthians 11:1 (NIV)

Focus Daily: (Read the above verse.)

Focus Questions: The apostle Paul gave this message to the Corinthian church. How does that apply to you and me as individuals? How does that challenge you?

Practice Daily: Remember, as always, our posture in these practices is to create space for intimacy with God and with other people. Love is always the context. Spend some time in prayer today asking God whom you could mentor. It could be as simple as someone with whom you regularly have lunch, or it could be someone that you will intentionally check in with every couple of days. You should be praying intentionally for that person and looking for the opportunity to more directly invest in him or her. You may already have that relationship established, or you may not. Write down this person's name in your journal entry.

JOURNAL DAILY

(Write at least three sentences per day):

_____

_____

_____

_____

_____

_____

_____

_____

_____

_____

_____

_____

_____

_____

_____

_____

_____

_____

Jesus Mentored

MEMORIZE WEEKLY

Follow my example, as I follow the example of Christ.
—1 Corinthians 11:1 (NIV)

Focus Daily: "For I received from the Lord what I also passed on to you" (1 Corinthians 11:23 NIV).

Focus Questions: What have you received from the Lord? What impact has Jesus had on your life?

Practice Daily: Write down the name of the person you identified yesterday. Where is the common ground in your relationship? What aspect of your relationship with Christ is something that would resonate with them?

JOURNAL DAILY

(Write at least three sentences per day):

Jesus Mentored

Follow my example, as I follow the example of Christ.
—1 Corinthians 11:1 (NIV)

Focus Daily: "Follow God's example, therefore, as dearly loved children and walk in the way of love, just as Christ loved us and gave himself up for us" (Ephesians 5:1–2 NIV).

Focus Questions: What does it look like for you to "walk in the way of love"? What are some small ways and some big ways that you can "give yourself up" in His name?

Practice Daily: Make an appointment with your chosen person. Do this with the intention of discovering the nature of his or her relationship with God. What are a couple simple, noninvasive questions you could ask them? Write those in today's journal entry.

JOURNAL DAILY
(Write at least three sentences per day):

_____

_____

_____

_____

_____

_____

_____

_____

_____

_____

_____

_____

_____

_____

_____

_____

_____

Jesus Mentored

MEMORIZE WEEKLY

Follow my example, as I follow the example of Christ.
—1 Corinthians 11:1 (NIV)

Focus Daily: "I no longer call you servants, because a servant does not know his master's business. Instead, I have called you friends, for everything that I learned from my Father I have made known to you" (John 15:15 NIV).

Focus Questions: Jesus is speaking to His immediate group of disciples in the above verse. How does this verse speak to the common ground between Jesus and the disciples?

Practice Daily: How would you describe your person's relationship with God based on your interaction? What next steps do you think he or she needs to take with Jesus? Write your answers in today's journal entry.

JOURNAL DAILY

(Write at least three sentences per day):

Jesus Mentored

MEMORIZE WEEKLY

Follow my example, as I follow the example of Christ.
—1 Corinthians 11:1 (NIV)

Focus Daily: "Freely you have received; freely give" (Matthew 10:8b NIV).

Focus Questions: As you contemplate the life change you have experienced in Christ, how does that motivate you to share your story? Have you ever thought of it in that regard?

Practice Daily: Thinking back to yesterday's focus verse how can you share "everything you have learned from the Father" with your person? Our responsibility isn't necessarily to fill the other person's cup but to empty our own cup. You have your own journey with Jesus to share. Don't feel like you need to be more mature than you are. What are three key experiences in your relationship with God that you could share with your person? Write them in bullet points in today's journal entry.

JOURNAL DAILY

(Write at least three sentences per day):

_____

_____

_____

_____

_____

_____

_____

_____

_____

_____

_____

_____

_____

_____

_____

_____

_____

_____

Jesus Mentored

MEMORIZE WEEKLY
Follow my example, as I follow the example of Christ.
—1 Corinthians 11:1 (NIV)

Focus Daily: "Then Jesus came to them and said, 'All authority in heaven and on earth has been given to me. Therefore go and make disciples of all nations, baptizing them in the name of the Father and of the Son and of the Holy Spirit, and teaching them to obey everything I have commanded you. And surely I am with you always, to the very end of the age'" (Matthew 28:18–20 NIV).

Focus Questions: Jesus is asking us to go and make disciples, who will go and make disciples, and so on. That is the heart of mentoring. What do you think He meant when he said, "I am with you always, to the very end of the age"?

Practice Daily: Make an appointment with your person within the next two weeks with the intention of sharing one or two of the key points in your story you shared in yesterday's practice. Also, pray about the next steps you believe your person needs to take in his or her journey with Jesus. Pray for the opportunity and the timing to share those thoughts with him or her. This is just the beginning of your mentoring relationship. Pray that God guides you as you meet your person on common ground and that you lead by example. As you follow Jesus, you can encourage him or her to walk with you. At the end of the day, that is where the most powerful mentoring will occur.

JOURNAL DAILY

(Write at least three sentences per day):

_____

_____

_____

_____

_____

_____

_____

_____

_____

_____

_____

_____

_____

_____

Jesus Rested

Six days a week we wrestle with the world, wringing
profit from the earth; on the Sabbath we especially
care for the seed of eternity planted in the soul. The
world has our hands, but our soul belongs to Someone
Else.
—Abraham Joshua Heschel

Resting in Christ is about identity. The identity that rests in Him
no longer has to prove itself. We don't have to prove ourselves to
anyone because we are loved and accepted and qualified by the
work of someone else who is far more qualified to the task. It is what He
says about us that is most true. And he says, "You are loved." He says, "You
are my child." He says that we are eternal beings of infinite worth. He says
we have something to offer the world. And He says that we can live with
purpose, hope, and meaning.

This is where we can rest. That is where we can find peace.

> "Peace I leave with you; my peace I
> give you. I do not give to you as the
> world gives. Do not let your hearts be
> troubled and do not be afraid."
>
> **(John 14:27 NIV)**

The world doesn't give us peace. At least not the kind of peace that restores our souls. It is tough for the soul continually striving to be at peace. The world says we are more valuable when we are hurried and busy. The world says our importance is directly related to our productivity, among other things. "What do you bring to the table? Are you pleasant to look at? Are you funny? Are you powerful? What have you achieved?" And we believe that when we answer these questions correctly, we will be happy and at peace. But the truth is, these are very delicate, volatile things that can vanish in a heartbeat, leaving us anxious and empty and wondering if we matter at all.

Israel spent four hundred years as slaves to the Egyptians. They spent four hundred years being told that their value was only in how they produced for their masters. Seven days a week, they worked to prove to the Egyptians and possibly to themselves that they should take up space on this planet. More bricks equated to another day of life and another meal to sustain a struggling family.

But when God delivered the Israelites through Moses, He took them into the wilderness to detox them from four hundred years of slavery. He was going to teach them how to be a people. And more importantly, He was going to show them where their identities are genuinely grounded. This is even more apparent when God granted Israel the law and rest was among the top ten commandments: "Remember the Sabbath day by keeping it holy. Six days you shall labor and do all your work, but the seventh day is a sabbath to the LORD your God. On it you shall not do any work" (Exodus 20:8–10 NIV).

Why was this so important that it rose all the way to the top of priorities on God's mind? They still needed to work. They still needed to be productive. They still needed to be good stewards of what they had been given. But at the same time, they were commanded to rest, so God lovingly directed them to break from the busyness and the hurry. He tells all of us that we are more than humans *doing*; we are humans *being*. Our value isn't attached to what we produce. Our value, our identities, are grounded entirely in the reality of His love. Nothing else. Nothing more.

What He says about us and what He intends for us is enough. He made us in order to love us and to find ourselves in loving Him.

The more we allow that truth to penetrate our hearts, the more peace we are going to find. And in that peace our productivity has meaning and our work is infused with purpose. Because the whole of our lives is infused with our created purpose. And in that, there is joy. In His rest, the work is elevated. God gives this command to His people to remind them every seven days who they are. It reminds them that their work doesn't define them and it doesn't own them.

> "The LORD is my shepherd; I shall not want. He makes me lie down in green pastures. He leads me beside still waters. He restores my soul."
>
> **(Psalm 23:1–3 ESV)**

Rest in Christ is about restoration. The human soul is a delicate thing. It is worn down by the hurriedness and burden of life. We can't will it to restoration. It can't be manipulated. Doing more of the same won't give it a rest. The only way the soul is restored is when it is still. The psalmist equated people with sheep. All sheep do is eat and sleep. The sheep unwaveringly and innocently trust the shepherd as he leads them into stillness. They follow Him to the place where there is no striving and there is no anxiety. They feel safe because they know who watches over them.

Are you soul weary? Do you carry that burden of spirit that weighs you down even when circumstances are favorable? You're busy and productive. Perhaps you are succeeding at everything you set your sights on. And still, you are dissatisfied and exhausted. Your days off are filled with any number of distractions. You may entertain yourself endlessly. Or you may feel obligated to do all the things around the house that seem neglected. You may even feel guilty when you are not working on something. Listen

to the words of our Hero: "Come to me, all you who are weary and burdened, and I will give you rest. Take my yoke upon you and learn from
me, for I am gentle and humble in heart, and you will find rest for your
souls" (Matthew 11:28–29 NIV).

The Good Shepherd is saying, "Come away with me. Be at peace. Follow in my footsteps and my rhythm of life. There's a time to work and
engage fully in the world around you. And there is a time just to be. Let
me love you in the stillness. Let me love you in the silence. Let me restore
your soul."

We also find this in the Gospel of Mark: "Then, because so many people were coming and going that they did not even have a chance to eat, he
said to them, 'Come with me by yourselves to a quiet place and get some
rest" (Mark 6:31 NIV).

We find Jesus observing the Sabbath rhythms and encouraging His
disciples to do so as well. We see Him coming apart from the crowds
very often to be still and restored. He sought out that quiet time with
His Father and then entered back into the fray of life. We even see Him
taking a nap in the middle of a boat trip much to the dismay of His disciples. A storm came up, and His disciples were full of anxiety. They were
alarmed that He wasn't more alarmed. Jesus was sleeping so deeply the
storm didn't even wake Him.

Sometimes the best choice we can make is to get a nap. Because the
storm will wake us soon enough.

It is in our nature to take something that is supposed to be helpful and turn it into a competition. "Who is the best person at observing
Sabbath. Who is just crushing rest?" The legalists of ancient Israel had
become particularly good at taking a simple thing and making it complicated. They added so many rules on top of the Sabbath that it was more
work to rest than it was to work: "Then [Jesus] said to them, 'The Sabbath
was made for man, not man for the Sabbath'" (Mark 2:27 NIV).

Jesus reminds us all why we step away with Him. The Sabbath, the
rest, is meant to lift the burden of life, not add to it.

The tide goes in, and the tide goes out. There is a time for us to work with all our might. But it is in our design to step away and rest. The soul rest we have in Jesus doesn't just restore our energy reserves. It restores our identities. It makes whole what has been chipped away by the struggle of life. His rest regularly tells us who we are and whose we are. He restores, realigns, and recalibrates all that is crushed in our hurriedness.

DAY 1

Jesus Rested

MEMORIZE WEEKLY

*Come to me, all you who are weary and burdened,
and I will give you rest. Take my yoke upon you
and learn from me, for I am gentle and humble
in heart, and you will find rest for your souls.*
—Matthew 11:28–29 (NIV)

Focus Daily: (Read the above verse.)

Focus Questions: When have you felt you were the most soul tired?
What were the circumstances surrounding it? What did you do?

Practice Daily: Remember, as always, our posture in these practices is to
create space for intimacy with God and with other people. Love is always
the context. If you don't normally have a Sabbath routine, pick a day
of the week that makes sense in your life rhythm. What kinds of things
will you do on your Sabbath that restore your soul? Write the answers in
today's journal entry.

JOURNAL DAILY

(Write at least three sentences per day):

_____

_____

_____

_____

_____

_____

_____

_____

_____

_____

_____

_____

_____

_____

_____

_____

_____

Jesus Rested

MEMORIZE WEEKLY

Come to me, all you who are weary and burdened, and I will give you rest. Take my yoke upon you and learn from me, for I am gentle and humble in heart, and you will find rest for your souls.
—Matthew 11:28–29 (NIV)

Focus Daily: "Remember the Sabbath day by keeping it holy. Six days you shall labor and do all your work, but the seventh day is a sabbath to the LORD your God. On it you shall not do any work" (Exodus 20:8–10 NIV).

Focus Questions: Is it difficult for you to "turn off" for a whole day? What are you tempted to do on a Sabbath that you would consider work?

Practice Daily: Make a plan for the Sabbath day you picked yesterday. What will you do to rest and restore in Christ?

JOURNAL DAILY

(Write at least three sentences per day):

Jesus Rested

MEMORIZE WEEKLY

Come to me, all you who are weary and burdened, and I will give you rest. Take my yoke upon you and learn from me, for I am gentle and humble in heart, and you will find rest for your souls.
—Matthew 11:28–29 (NIV)

Focus Daily: "The LORD is my shepherd; I shall not want. He makes me lie down in green pastures. He leads me beside still waters. He restores my soul" (Psalm 23:1–3 ESV).

Focus Questions: When was the last time you were "still?" What does that look like?

Practice Daily: Finding your rest doesn't have to be just a Sabbath day. It is healthy to set aside quiet moments in your day when you can just be still and be present with Jesus. When is there a natural break in your work routine for a few moments like this? Write it down in today's journal entry. Make a plan for one five-minute "still water" moment for each remaining day of the week. Consider praying through Psalm 23 in those windows of time.

JOURNAL DAILY

(Write at least three sentences per day):

_____

_____

_____

_____

_____

_____

_____

_____

_____

_____

_____

_____

_____

_____

_____

_____

_____

Jesus Rested

MEMORIZE WEEKLY

Come to me, all you who are weary and burdened,
and I will give you rest. Take my yoke upon you
and learn from me, for I am gentle and humble
in heart, and you will find rest for your souls.
—Matthew 11:28–29 (NIV)

Focus Daily: "Come with me by yourselves to a quiet place and get some rest" (Mark 6:31 NIV).

Focus Questions: Where is a restorative place for you? How long do you have to stay there before you feel rested?

Practice Daily: When is your next vacation? Have you ever come back from vacation more tired than when you started? Start making plans for your next vacation with soul rest in mind as the primary goal. Write some ideas down today.

JOURNAL DAILY

(Write at least three sentences per day):

_____

_____

_____

_____

_____

_____

_____

_____

_____

_____

_____

_____

_____

_____

_____

_____

_____

Jesus Rested

MEMORIZE WEEKLY

Come to me, all you who are weary and burdened,
and I will give you rest. Take my yoke upon you
and learn from me, for I am gentle and humble
in heart, and you will find rest for your souls.
—Matthew 11:28–29 (NIV)

Focus Daily: "By the seventh day God had finished the work he had been doing; so on the seventh day he rested from all his work. Then God blessed the seventh day and made it holy, because on it he rested from all the work of creating that he had done" (Genesis 2:2–3 NIV).

Focus Questions: The Sabbath rhythm is a reflection of God's creation rhythm. Why do you think God rested on the seventh day?

Practice Daily: Have you ever taken a day off from work just because you're tired? If you are feeling that way now, write down the date when you will use a vacation day just for soul restoration.

JOURNAL DAILY

(Write at least three sentences per day):

Jesus Rested

MEMORIZE WEEKLY

Come to me, all you who are weary and burdened, and I will give you rest. Take my yoke upon you and learn from me, for I am gentle and humble in heart, and you will find rest for your souls.
—Matthew 11:28–29 (NIV)

Focus Daily: "Let us, therefore, make every effort to enter that rest, so that no one will perish by following their example of disobedience" (Hebrews 4:11 NIV).

Focus Questions: In Hebrews, the author gives the example God's rest in creation and the rest He ultimately provides through salvation to the believer. So the Sabbath rest also points to a much larger picture than mere physical rest. It points to the ultimate restoration of all creation. How can you keep that reminder in front of you when you practice your own Sabbath?

Practice Daily: As you enter into your Sabbath rest, pray through these three things: Remember who you are in Christ. Remember that it is Jesus who restores your soul as you are "still" with Him. And remember that the Sabbath rest points beyond itself to the fruition of God's Kingdom when heaven comes to earth and God restores everything to its original wholeness. Write about the experience in today's journal entry.

JOURNAL DAILY

(Write at least three sentences per day):

_____

_____

_____

_____

_____

_____

_____

_____

_____

_____

_____

_____

_____

_____

_____

_____

_____

Conclusion

As we journey with Jesus, we should revisit the practices we've covered many times. And as we seek to imitate our Hero, we will inevitably find ourselves in these sacred spaces. These practices create space in our lives for more intimacy with God and with the people He loves. We can come back to them in different ways, but our framework of loving God and loving others must remain the same. When we keep these things as the highest priority, the practices have soul and sustainability. Without that framework, they are just another form of legalism. We must always remember that that these practices are meant to grow, enrich, and restore our souls instead of further loading them down.

So revisit these practices often, keeping in mind that all of them should be practiced some of the time and none of them should be practiced all of the time. Like any relationship, the tide goes in and out, and we will have seasons when we should emphasize some practices over others. It may entail going back to the beginning and starting over, it may require more than a week on a specific practice, or it may mean that the questions and exercises need to be explored more thoroughly than the first time. But no matter how the journey continues, know that it will be transformational.

Just as this entire experience is meant to be a starter, a beginning, to living life more like Jesus, it is also meant to help us imitate the regular rhythm of His life in the Gospels. It is in no way comprehensive. The life of our Hero is richer than any of us dare to comprehend. As our relationship with Him grows, our understanding of His wisdom, His beauty, and His love will grow as well. Because moving toward Him is the only way to fall more in love with Him, and in that love, we look more and more like Jesus, carrying us to the day we finally see our Hero face to face.

WALKING HAND IN HAND AS CHRIST'S LOVE
transforms lives

MEETING THE
DEEPEST NEEDS

WE BELIEVE THE GOSPEL IS TRANSFORMATIVE

And you can change the world one child at a time.

Thousands of children in the world are born into a cycle of poverty that has been around for generations, leaving them without hope for a safe and secure future. For a little more than $1 a day you can provide the tools a child needs to break the cycle in the name of Jesus.

OUR CONTACT

📞 423-894-6060
✉️ info@amginternational.org

📷 @amgintl
📍 6815 Shallowford Rd. Chattanooga, TN 37421

Made in the USA
Middletown, DE
16 April 2023

28854908R00130